ACCIDENTALLY IN CHARGE

A BUSINESS BOOK FOR PEOPLE WHO HATE BUSINESS BOOKS

JOSH BLACK

First published by Ultimate World Publishing 2025
Copyright © 2025 Josh Black

ISBN

Paperback: 978-1-923425-81-1
Ebook: 978-1-923425-82-8

Cover design: Ultimate World Publishing
Layout and typesetting: Ultimate World Publishing
Editor: James Salmon

Ultimate World Publishing
Diamond Creek,
Victoria Australia 3089
www.writeabook.com.au

DEDICATION

For Vinny... You took an extra two weeks to arrive, which was exactly what I needed to get this book done. Perfect timing.

CONTENTS

FOREWORD

WHY YOU'RE PROBABLY HOLDING THIS BOOK

Business books can be handy if you've suddenly found yourself running the show instead of on the tools. But the reality is that most of them won't resonate with a lot of people. This isn't written by someone who went to Oxford or feels like they're starting on level 100. This book's for the ones figuring it out as they go. It's about what actually happens... the messy bits, the wrong turns, and what you learn when things don't go to plan. Most business books are dry as toast. If nothing else, I hope this one gives you a laugh. Might as well have a bit of fun while you learn.

When it comes to reading this book, think of it less as a rigid guide and more as a collection of lessons meant to be lived...one day at a time. Its origins were humble, to say the least. It all started with the notes app on my phone. Back then, the intent was simple: to get better at trivia. I'd jot down random facts...bits of knowledge I'd come across that I figured might give me an edge on Wednesday night trivia at The Rochester Hotel. I still haven't crushed it there, but I do know that Henry VIII had six wives and beheaded two, the dartboard line is called an oche, black pepper and cumin are the two best-selling peppers, and the Cambodian alphabet is the longest in the world with seventy-six letters. This information has never won me a free pint, but who knows? Maybe one day, right?

But eventually, something started to shift. The notes evolved beyond trivia and into quotes I'd read, little nuggets of wisdom that stuck with me, and eventually, reflections of my own experiences. Before long, the notes weren't just about winning pub trivia...they were about navigating life. And that's when the real value emerged.

I started transferring these lessons into PowerPoint slides (so corporate of me), organising them into something I could actually use. Every morning, I'd sit down, open my laptop, and just read one slide. Whatever the lesson was, that became my focus for the day. And it wasn't just theoretical...I made sure to live it. The format of this book is built around those slides, but with a twist. Each chapter starts with a single lesson...something clear and actionable. But the real meat is in the story that follows, where I explained how I learned it.

I recall one day, I read a slide about avoiding the 'ostrich approach' to conflict...you know, burying your head in the sand and hoping a problem will magically disappear. It hit me like a ton of bricks because I was deep in avoidance mode at the time. I had a tough conversation looming over me, one I'd been dodging for weeks. But reading that slide gave me the push I needed. I stopped avoiding, confronted the issue, and walked away feeling lighter, more capable.

That's the thing about these lessons...they almost always apply to something you're going through. And the more you live them, the more ingrained they become. Over time, you don't just get better at handling challenges...you start to anticipate them, navigate them, and grow for them in ways you didn't think were possible.

WHY YOU'RE PROBABLY HOLDING THIS BOOK

Eventually, this daily ritual sparked an idea. At the time, my 23-year-old brother and one of his mates were working with Paint It Black and started to take more responsibility and learn the ropes of project and people management. I wanted to give them something tangible...a document of lessons I wish I'd known at their age. What started as slides for my own growth became something bigger.

So, whether you picked this up because you're leading a team, sick of corporate buzzwords, or just here for the funny stories, I hope you find something useful in these pages. And if nothing else, at least you'll walk away with some useless trivia.

INTRO

A LEADERSHIP BOOK FOR THE REST OF US

Welcome to the wild, beautiful chaos of business leadership.

Let's get one thing straight off the bat: I am no guru. I've screwed up more times than I can count...and if we're being honest, I'll screw up again. These lessons aren't about painting some flawless picture of success. There's no magic formula here, no blueprint for perfection. This is more like a survival guide for anyone brave... or foolish enough...to step into the arena every day, roll up their sleeves, and have a crack at it.

But here's what gets me: for a country built on small businesses, we don't get much of a say in the leadership conversation. I've been to plenty of business events, industry conferences, and leadership panels, and they all seem to be aimed at corporate execs. The speakers come from different backgrounds, sure...diverse in gender, culture, experience, but when it comes to the jobs they've held, they're all cut from the same cloth. They talk about restructuring departments, managing shareholders, and leading global teams. They refer to HR teams, recruitment teams, strategy teams, payroll teams...when you start a small business... it's a one-man team, wearing multiple hats.

And that's crazy, because small businesses make up 97% of all businesses in this country and contribute over half a trillion dollars to the economy. We are the backbone of this place, yet when it comes to leadership advice, we're stuck trying to apply lessons from Fortune 500 companies that have nothing to do with the realities we face.

That's where this book comes in.

This isn't a leadership book for boardroom warriors...it's for the small business owners who suddenly find themselves running the show, who are making it up as they go, and the people who never saw themselves as 'leaders' but somehow ended up in charge. Even though a lot of the lessons are written with trades in mind, they apply to anyone who's had to figure out leadership on the fly.

Writing all this down hasn't made me an expert. Far from it. Most days, I still feel like I'm winging it. But this book has become a bit of a compass...something to come back to when things feel uncertain, a reminder of the core values that make my company, Paint It Black, what it is. Do we hit the mark every time? Absolutely not. But with these lessons in mind, we're getting closer than we ever could without them.

Now, I'll be honest...writing something even remotely 'self-help' makes me feel like a bit of a fraud. This isn't a book of answers, and it's not me claiming to have it all worked out. If anything, it's a record of what I've learned so far and the mistakes I've made along the way. It's for the young leaders at Paint It Black who are stepping up, but it's also for anyone out there wondering if they're cut out for leadership or running a business.

One thing that has always stuck with me is something Jeff Bezos calls the 'regret minimization framework'. When faced with a tough decision, he imagines himself twenty years down the track and asks: "What decision will I regret less?" More often than not, the answer isn't, "I wish I'd played it safe". That idea has always resonated with me...not because it's revolutionary, but because it's simple. It pushes you toward courage.

At the very least, I hope this book gives you a laugh. It's part of our ethos at Paint It Black: take what you do seriously but never take yourself too seriously. Reflecting on the first decade of the business has been equal parts humbling and hilarious.

Cricket legend Kerry O'Keefe once said that everyone should write their own book, even if it's just for themselves. That's how this started...for me, for our team, for the next generation of leaders figuring things out in real-time. It's not perfect. Take from it what you will.

If you're part of Paint It Black, this is our story. If you're not, I hope you find something useful in here...whether it's a lesson, a laugh, or just a reminder that no one has all the answers. Because at the end of the day, this is a book for the imperfect...the ones figuring it out, one mistake at a time.

And now, let's get into how it all started.

PROLOGUE

BUY THE TICKET, TAKE THE RIDE

It had been almost a year since I'd ditched my bed frame for a more inconspicuous mattress on the floor. Yes, at first it was a temporary solution while I searched for the perfect bed...but I'd grown to like its modest appeal. There was something charming about a mattress on the floor. Kind of looked like a guy who was starting to lose his shit...I liked that.

The room only got natural daylight through a skylight for two hours a day. My office was a walnut Ikea desk, in the corner of my bedroom. It sat on a light grey, dirty carpet; knotted, synthetic, which you would never dare take your socks off on. A classic share house in the Melbourne suburb of Kensington. Picture the quintessential Kensington street; rows of double-fronted Victorian terraces with intricate iron lacework, steep roofs, and tall windows standing proudly amidst tree-lined avenues...well we didn't have one of those houses.

Compared to the previous share house though, it was the Taj Mahal. After completing my painting apprentice I'd spent a typical two years living in London, living in a modest shack that was one of a street full of identical poorly rendered two-story shoeboxes. At any one time there was anything between six and fourteen people living in that three-bedroom house. We crammed them in wherever we could...couches, under the staircase, in the cubby house, on the floor...whatever we could do to lessen the rent. We were in South Wimbledon. Not up on Wimbledon hill, overlooking the luscious fairways of the exclusive Wimbledon Golf Club. Beautifully carved around a graceful lake, occupied by colossal swans and ducks, especially picturesque on a motionless winter's morning. Nope, nowhere near there...we lived south of the village, where too often the morning air is filled with mist, everything is grey, the clouds are low. There's no perspective. You can't see above any buildings, there's no horizon. A fox was forever rummaging through the rubbish that lined our street. The painted wallpaper was peeling, revealing the cracked concrete walls....but we didn't give a shit; we were having the time of our lives.

Our Kensington share house was decent, as far as share houses go. A bit of peeling paint here, a mysterious squeaking floorboard there, but overall, liveable. For me, though, it would've been a whole lot better if I hadn't lost that bloody FIFA tournament on the PlayStation. It was supposed to be a friendly competition, a little Sunday night entertainment with the boys after we'd demolished a pile of greasy burgers that left our hands slick with oil and the air thick with the aroma of charred beef. The stakes? The best room in the house.

We decided to randomise team selection...pure chaos. FIFA's version of Russian roulette. I hit the button and watched in horror as the Yeovil Town logo flashed onto the screen. Yeovil, a struggling Division two team with players who ran like they had concrete in their boots. Meanwhile, my housemates, smug as ever, drew Manchester City and Barcelona. The odds couldn't have been more stacked. My earlier dominance in friendlies counted for nothing now. It was David vs Goliath, only this time, Goliath had Lionel Messi and Kevin De Bruyne.

The game started with the faint hum of the PlayStation fan in the background, punctuated by the occasional rattle of passing trains outside. My sweaty fingers slipped on the controller as I tried to wrangle Yeovil's background into something resembling a defence. The guys cackled as Barcelona's forwards danced around my defenders, weaving through like a hot knife through butter. Manchester City's midfield was unstoppable...every tackle I attempted seemed to bounce back to them like they were magnetised to the ball.

I managed a consolation goal in the match for the worst room of the house...a scrappy mess of a corner that bobbled into the net... but it was too little, too late. The final whistle blew, and the room erupted in laughter. The smell of victory...or in my case, greasy defeat...hung in the air. And so, it was decided: I got the smallest, darkest room in the house. Half the size of the others, no windows, and not even a balcony to compensate. It was little more than a glorified storage closet.

But that room, dingy and cramped...would become the birth of Paint It Black HQ.

It was 2015 when I took the leap of faith into the unknown. Up until then, my weekends had been filled with cash-in-hand jobs for mates. A bit of painting here, a quick reno touch-up there. Decent top up to my full-time job, but just a bit of a side hustle. Then, out of nowhere, a contact suggested I tender for a project: nine luxury townhouses in Brighton. Nine. Luxury. Townhouses. Brighton. I didn't even know where to start, but something inside me whispered, why not?

I didn't have an ABN. I didn't understand GST or BAS. Taxes were a foreign concept to me. All I knew was how to paint. But the idea of working on a project of that scale? It was magnetic.

I sat at my tiny desk in my shoebox room, surrounded by half-empty coffee cups and the faint smell of turps hanging to my work clothes, staring at the plans. The drawings might as well have been hieroglyphics. I went over them again. And again. And again. The pages were thick and smelled faintly of fresh ink, the crisp edges softening with every turn. I studied every line, every symbol, every note scribbled in the margins, until I could read the specifications in my sleep.

I knew the underground services like the back of my hand... stormwater, electrical conduits, sewerage layouts. But did I need to? Absolutely not. I just didn't know what I was doing and was worried I'd miss something. Miss what exactly? A drain that needed painting? I look back now and laugh as I only need about four out of one hundred pages in a plan set. I probably knew as much about that project as the architect. Every detail gave me a small boost of confidence though, a feeling that maybe, just maybe I could pull this off.

The tender process was a whirlwind of confusion. I had no idea how to price a job like this. I spent hours researching, trying to figure out how to account for labour, materials, overheads – what was an overhead? I didn't sleep much that week, sitting in the glow of my laptop as I Googled terms like 'progress claims' and 'retentions'.

When I finally hit send on the tender submission, without a capability statement or plan, just my word that I'd do a good job, it felt surreal. I had no idea if I'd priced it correctly or if I'd missed something critical. I thought the person accepting my tender would laugh at a mistake I'd made. But there was a quiet pride knowing I'd done everything I could.

Looking back, that FIFA loss was a blessing in disguise. The tiny, windowless room forced me to focus, to strip away distractions and dream of building a business in Brighton. It shouldn't have worked. But sometimes, all it takes is a leap...and a little blind faith.

I had tried to learn a few things about business the year previous. I was working as a painter on commercial sites, mostly in the CBD. The job itself was about as fun as eating burnt toast, but it did teach me a lot about commercial painting. It also helped me to quickly realise that eating burnt toast wasn't what I wanted to do for too long and was the catalyst for enrolling in a night course in business management course at RMIT university. For the most part, the biggest thing I got out of that was a student concession card. I ended up going to South America for a couple of months in the middle of that course and never went back...I'll just learn on the run!

Somehow, I won the tender (most likely under quoted). Suddenly, Paint It Black wasn't just a weekend hustle. I bought a few extra tools, crammed them under the staircase in the share house and found myself with a team...an apprentice who was looking for a job because he'd fucked up and crashed his car into a BMW drunk and my ol' mate Rab. We weren't exactly built for the job, but we didn't let that stop us. We dove in headfirst with nothing but bravado and an alarming level of ignorance.

Looking back, it was a baptism of fire...the ultimate learning experience. My strategy was simple...surround myself with the right people and absorb every bit of knowledge I could. My sister Hannah, a natural choice for designing our logo, was studying visual merchandising at the time. The best part? She was willing to do it for free.

I also had a stroke of luck when my old footy coach, who had probably felt a twinge of guilt for dropping me a few too many times during my playing days at Colac, stepped in to help. He was an accountant, and with his assistance, we got the business off the ground.

Being a devout Rolling Stones fan, the name Paint It Black was an obvious choice, a perfect fit for the madness I was about to unleash.

It was chaotic, exhilarating and terrifying. But that leap of faith taught me more about business, and myself, than any amount of planning ever could.

Over the years, we've had the privilege of working on some remarkable projects...at the time of writing I've just come from a job in Toorak...an absolute temple of excess. The grand entryway alone is two stories high, with marble floors that go from $5,000 per tile. African blackwood panelling lines the study, bookshelves stretching from floor to ceiling like something out of a billionaire's dream library. Morning light pours through colossal glass windows, burnishing every corner in a warm, golden glow. The French architraves? $8,000 a piece. And then there's the pendant light...a singular masterpiece hanging directly above the living room, worth a casual $130,000. Oh, and the pantry? It's roughly the same size as our apartment in Collingwood.

It's a house I've got no business being in, really, but this line of work has opened doors to places and people I could never imagine.

We've painted theme parks where roller coasters thundered past as we worked, the scent of hot churros and sunscreen hanging in the air. We got a prison shut down when one of our painters dropped his putty knife and sent the place into a full lockdown until it was found. We painted bridges, where the world roared beneath our feet, cars zooming by like angry hornets below.

And then there were the clients. Most have been incredible, like comedian Andy Lee, who's just as funny a person as you'd hope for, or footy legend Brian Taylor, whose booming voice could carry across the job site. At one point, we even painted the house of an acting Prime Minister.

But not every client has been a joy to work for. We've had our fair share of egos, micromanagers, and downright nightmares. Don't worry, we'll get to them in due course.

This work has brought me face-to-face with people from every walk of life, and it's been a rollercoaster. There was a client I made cry...not because of a botched job, but because I complimented her house. She broke down right there, telling me about her divorce and how the house felt like her last piece of stability. Then there was the time I copped a one-star Google review for parking on someone's curb.

We've had moments of triumph, too. We've won awards that made me step back and think, maybe we're doing something right here. And we've had the absurd...like the time one of our workers ended up on the news while on the job, or the day my car got stolen, adding another chapter to the chaos that seems to follow.

And, of course, there's a certain poetry in the fact that, years after starting my own business, I found myself in the position of sacking my own boss. A full-circle moment that was as traumatic as it was surreal.

This was just the beginning. There were more stories – of workers who became great friends, clients who tested every ounce of patience, and projects that pushed us to our limits. But for now, I'm reminded of how far we've come. From losing a game of FIFA to painting the acting Prime Minister's house. Life's funny like that.

CHAPTER 1

STIRRING UP BOOMERS

Dealing with criticism is one of the toughest aspects of putting yourself out there, especially in Australia. There's a lot to love about our culture...its laid-back attitude, sense of humour, and the emphasis on mateship. But lurking in the shadows is the tall poppy syndrome, the tendency to cut people down when they start standing out too much. It's a cultural quirk that can feel suffocating if you're trying to push boundaries or do something different. The message is often clear...don't get too big for your boots.

Contrast this with American culture, where success is celebrated... even exaggerated. Their hyper-enthusiasm can sometimes feel over the top, but it's the opposite of our tendency to downplay achievements. Americans often put the individual first, where the narrative is about personal triumph and being the best, even above the team. It's a different beast entirely. Somewhere between the two lies the sweet spot: a culture that celebrates success and encourages people to strive for greatness while staying grounded and humble. A team-first mentality is valuable, but it shouldn't come at the expense of stifling ambition.

In a perfect world, you'd have the humility of an Australian mindset balanced with the celebratory nature of the American ethos. Celebrate people for having a go but temper it with a healthy dose of humility.

We've seen this tension play out in sports. Take Hawthorn footballer Jack Ginnivan as an example. He's part of this new-age wave of players...active on TikTok, full of personality, and seemingly immune to what people think about him. He stirs up the boomers, but at the same time, plays with a team-first attitude and delivers when it matters. Why do we look down on players like him for having a personality? Do we want robots out there? Hawthorn has embraced who he is, and Ginnivan has paid them back tenfold on the field... and membership sales.

It's the same with Australia's new test batter, Sam Konstas. He comes out in front of 90,000 at the MCG for his first game, plays some aggressive shots, interacts with the crowd, and even nearly gets in a fight with India's superstar, Virat Kohli. Again, the boomers lose their minds: *Keep your mouth shut, play some forward defence, earn some respect.* But Konstas had a plan. He put the team first, executed with brash nineteen-year-old confidence, and helped Australia win. You could see he was having the time of his life...isn't living out your dream meant to be fun? Let them play, let them have a personality and let them upset the boomers. If they are team first and humble afterwards (and both Ginnivan and Konstas were), I say play on.

Criticism, however, often follows personalities like Ginnivan and Konstas. If you go looking for it, you'll always find some. Especially in the public eye, where salacious headlines dominate. You'll see something ridiculous like, *"Konstas Causes International Relations Disaster, Turns 1.5 Billion Indians Against Australia"*. Of course, I'll click on it, and it's just some washed-up old cricketer spouting nonsense...or worse, a quote from a 'fan' on Twitter. When did we start quoting fans as credible sources?

On a different level, it reminds me of Julia Gillard and the incredible respect I've gained for her over the years. She was an Australian Prime Minister with an arm tied behind her back...leading a minority government that requires constant compromise just to stay afloat. As the first female PM, she faced more scrutiny over what she wore and why she wasn't married with kids than all male Prime Ministers combined. She wanted to be known for her leadership and policies, not defined by her gender And yet, she had to endure constant attacks from people like Alan Jones and Tony Abbott, who didn't just critique her politics but weaponised her gender against her.

When Julia Gillard's father passed away, and Alan Jones said on air "he died in shame of his daughter," it's hard to fathom how she didn't bite back. But she waited, stayed composed, and eventually delivered her now famous misogyny speech...classy, calculated, and devastating. That speech wasn't just an answer to her critics; it was a masterclass in knowing whose opinions matter. She must have been exceptional at tuning out the noise and focusing on the voices that actually helped her lead. That kind of restraint, rising above the gutter, is something I can't help but admire.

On a smaller scale, the principle's the same. You might not have headlines written about you, *"Brush with the Law: Painter's Van Impounded for Parking on Local Man's Curb"*, or *"Paint It Black? More like Paint it Back! Pointer Accidentally Paints Entire House Wrong Colour, Sparks Neighbourhood Feud"*. The key is knowing which voices to listen to and which to tune out.

The challenge is how to filter criticism in a way that helps you grow instead of tearing you down. I always come back to the quote, *"If you're trying to appeal to everyone, by definition, you'll be putting out average work because you're aiming for the average person"*. Seth Godin, a renowned marketing expert, often emphasises the importance of focusing on a specific audience rather than attempting to please everyone. Similarly, the concept resonates with the idea that trying to please everyone often leads to mediocrity.

You can't please everyone and trying to will dilute your vision. Another favourite of mine is, "Don't take criticism off people you wouldn't ask advice from". That's been a game-changer. Build your own board of advisors...people whose opinions you trust and respect. Be selective with whose feedback you absorb, because if you try and respond to every bit of criticism, you'll drain yourself chasing other people's ideas of who you should be.

I also like to remind myself of a simple truth...communication happens on the listener's terms. Whether you're pitching an idea, delivering feedback, or defending yourself, the person on the other end determines how it lands. That principle helped with delivering any form of communication, but I've flipped it onto myself as well. If communication happens on the listener's terms, then I get to decide what feedback I take in. Unnecessary noise. Block it out. Focus on clarity, on what truly matters, and on the voice that helps you be better. Ultimately, it's about striking a balance: listening to constructive feedback, blocking out destructive noise, and staying true to what you're trying to achieve. It's tough, but if you're clear on your values and whose opinions matter, you'll find a way forward.

Man in the Arena

It's match day in Melbourne, and the city feels... alive. The CBD is a sea of scarves, every second person draped in their team's colours, from old school woollen classics to the modern, mass-produced variety. There's always the odd adult who hasn't grown out of wearing a full footy jumper, strutting around like they're warming up for the game themselves. Trams are packed shoulder-to-shoulder, voices buzzing with pre-game banter. As you get closer to the ground, the scent of hot chips wafts through the streets, mingling with the unmistakable smell of freshly steamed dim sims. Excitement hangs in the air, electric and contagious. The score is 0-0, no matter what your spot on the ladder, and for the next few hours, hope reigns supreme.

But it's more than just a game. It's about connection...families, work colleagues, siblings, and old mates bounded together by footy. The pubs are overflowing with optimism...today we've started at *The Standard Hotel,* in Fitzroy, pints clinking beneath walls plastered with framed gurneys and signed team posters. Conversation spills into the streets as fans predict blowouts or dream of miracle wins. It's not just about who wins or loses tonight; it's about the ritual, the community, and the shared stories that will be told long after the final siren.

So, I'm sitting behind the glass at Marvel Stadium with my best mate and brother. We've had enough beer to wash an elephant...maybe two...and my beloved Bulldogs are getting absolutely smashed by the Bombers. It's one of those nights where the footy Gods just don't smile your way.

As the game spirals out of control, the Bulldog faithful start turning on Bevo like he's the cause of all their life problems. "He can't coach!" "Why is Bailey Dale the sub?" someone shouts. "I just wish he'd be less...Bevo". I'm not even sure what that means, but in the heat of the moment, it sounds... profound.

Half time hits, and the scones come out. Now everyone's not only full of beer, but they've got a belly full of scones and opinions too. "Jamarra can't kick!" "Naughton needs to play defence!" "Our small forwards don't defend well enough!" The complaints are flowing faster than the beers, and let me tell you, I'm not immune to it either. I fire up the group chat and suddenly it's an avalanche of armchair coaches. Half of the opinions are my own incoherent ramblings.

Bont misses a goal, but he's practically untouchable. Even in the worst games, nobody dares say a bad word about the Bont. He's the footy equivalent of a sacred cow. So, we just silently pray for better days.

Later, I scroll through Twitter and it's knives out for Bevo and the Dogs. Meanwhile, across the pond, Pat Cummins is having a rare shocker in the Ashes, and every boomer on Twitter's got him pegged as Captain Woke. I'm biting my tongue, ready to go to war defending him. I mean, Bont and Pat are off limits, right? And then I'm not.

"It's a tough one, isn't it? You're in the public eye, someone asks you a question, and you know every single word that leaves your mouth is going to be cut up, reshaped, and plastered across headlines designed to trigger outrage. You can't win. It's a game of darts when you're on the board, and the public is lining up to take aim." I'm not sure who I'm speaking to, just in the direction of my mate and brother. "Pat's one of those rare athletes who speaks his mind, but only when he feels like he's educated on the subject. I've heard him talk about this before, if it's a topic he doesn't know much about, he'll keep his guard up, give a balanced, measured response, and avoid sticking his neck out. But if it's something he genuinely believes in, like climate change...you'll hear him talk about it with conviction, in a way that's thoughtful and respectful." I ramble on...the Bombers have kicked another two goals.

"He's never in your face about it, either. It's not *his way or the wrong way.* It's just what he believes. And yet, people lose their minds. What do they expect him to do? Toe the party line? Say nothing and just bowl on off stump? Heaven, forbid he has an opinion about the future of the planet while being one of the most influential athletes in the country." I'm now talking to the bartender, I think.

"Of course, then comes the critics...'*If he believes in global change so much, why does he fly to England to play cricket?*' Seriously? That's your take? Because he plays international cricket. Geez, there are some absolute fuckwits out there. It's like people forget that you can exist within a flawed system and still improve it." He's served me another beer, but his eyes are looking towards the bottles of water.

"It's the same with so many athletes or public figures who dare to say anything remotely outside the box. Look at Naomi Osaka, who spoke out about mental health, or Adam Goodes, who took a stand against racism. These are people who have achieved great things in their sports, but the second they open their mouths about something important, there's a line of people ready to tear them down. Why? Because it's easier to throw stones than it is to have a nuanced conversation."

The conversation (ramblings) continued in an underground cocktail bar. One of those places where you open a bookcase and are met with a pretentious vibe and menus in a font so fancy you can't read them. A couple of Negronis later, we'd solved all the Bulldogs problems and turned our attention to the rest of the world's issues.

By the time we left, we were clutching kebabs like they were lifeless, the greasy paper burning our fingers while garlic sauce dripped onto our shoes. The walk home was a blue of half-laughs, half-rants... It's amazing how a few beers, a bad game, and a passionate group of mates can do that to your perspective. You go from shouting criticisms into the void to realising that, at the end of the day, these people we hold to impossible standards are just like us... trying their best, doing what they think is right, and occasionally screwing up along the way.

The next morning, I woke up violently hungover, desperately afraid to move from the safety of my bed...groaning at the sunlight and my over-the-top footy analysis from the night before. It was just one bad game. Bevo knows what he's doing. We'll beat the Hawks next week. But, of course, I'd been swept up in the chaos, just like everyone else. And let's be real...it'll happen again.

But that's the thing about criticism, isn't it? Whether it's footy or business, it comes with the territory, and no matter how thick your skin is supposed to be, it can get under it. Running Paint It Black, I've faced my fair share. Clients, employees, even friends have had their opinions about how things should be done. And sometimes, even when you know it's coming from people who don't understand the pressure, it gets to you. You find yourself waking up the next morning, replaying those comments in your head, wondering if they were right, or if you're just taking it all too personally.

I've always wished I could just do my thing and not let other people's opinions bother me, but I've never been wired that way. It might stem back to my mum always telling me I played well in whatever sport I played. Even if I got a duck in cricket. "It was a good shot, there was just someone standing there that caught it." Criticism tends to get under my skin. Growing up playing footy, you get used to constructive criticism to a certain degree and in that environment, it mostly comes from a place to get better. But outside of that environment, when you put yourself out there... whether it's creating something or competing...people are going to criticise you. It's just part of the deal.

My business might be on a smaller scale, but I still feel the sting of criticism.

I'm not usually big on quotes – *there seems to be a lot of quotes in here so far for someone that is not big on them* – but there's one that really hit me when I first came across it, probably on a day when something trivial had gotten to me. It's Theodore Roosevelt's Man in the Arena speech in 1910. *"It is not the critic who counts; not the man who points out how the strong man stumbles, or where the doer of deeds could have done them better. The credit belongs to the man who is actually in the arena, whose face is marred by dust and sweat and blood; who strives valiantly; who errs, who comes short again and again; who spends himself in a worthy cause; who at the best knows in the end the triumph of high achievement, and who at the worst, if he fails, at least fails while daring greatly; so that his place shall never be with those cold and timid souls who neither know victory nor defeat."*

That speech stopped me in my tracks because it spoke right to the heart of what it means to put yourself out there. I've seen other people inspired by it too...Port Adelaide footballer Travis Boak has Man in the Arena written on his boots, and Hugh van Cuylenburg from the Resilience Project has it on his presentation clicker. The message resonates: if you're brave enough to step into the arena, criticism is inevitable. But if you're not in the fight with me, your feedback doesn't matter.

Over time, though, I've learned to sit with it. I'm not saying I've mastered the art of brushing it off completely...far from it...but I've gotten better at understanding where it's coming from. Not everyone's in the arena with you, fighting alongside you. Some are just in the stands, tossing out opinions with no real skin in the game. And while those voices can be loud, they don't matter as much as the ones who are in the trenches with you.

Now when criticism comes, I ask myself, who's saying this? Do they really get it? If the answer's no, I try to let it roll off. I'm still working on it, but it's a bit easier now to separate the noise from what really matters. And when I remind myself to listen only to those who are in the fight with me, I realise that the rest, well... it's just background chatter.

CHAPTER 2

I KILLED THE LAST PAINTER WHO WORKED HERE

The ethos 'don't be a dickhead' may sound blunt, but it's a core philosophy shared by high-performance teams like the All Blacks and Sydney Swans. It's not just a rule, but a mindset that emphasises humility, accountability, and respect.

For the All Blacks, who are world-renowned for their success, this concept is essential. They believe no one is bigger than the team and that greatness comes from doing the little things right, from cleaning up after yourself to staying grounded no matter how big the spotlight shines. Similarly, the Sydney Swans hold their players to this standard, ensuring everyone takes responsibility for their role and fosters a culture of humility and hard work.

At Paint It Black, we aim to follow that same ethos. Everyone takes ownership of their workspace, no one is above doing the basics, and ego is left at the door. Success, whether on the rugby field, the footy ground, or in business, comes from collaboration and leading by example, not arrogance or entitlement. The principle is simple, but it's this simplicity that makes it so powerful: don't be a dickhead.

It's about treating people with respect, doing your bit, and understanding that success isn't just about individual brilliance...it's about being a good teammate, staying humble, and working hard.

In the early days, living by the *'don't be a dickhead'* ethos was a real challenge. As the business started gaining traction and opportunities to grow came flooding in, I found myself struggling to keep up. Growth sounded pretty good in theory, but it forced me into some tough decisions. On the one hand, we had this incredible group of mates who were just starting their painting careers. They were raw but full of potential, energy, and enthusiasm. On the other hand, we desperately needed experienced hands to guide them.

We managed to hire a few seasoned painters. But it didn't take long to realise the experience came with strings attached. These were people that knew their craft...no doubt about it...but they weren't the kind of leaders we needed. They didn't embody our values, and that became a problem...fast. While they could produce high-quality work, they didn't inspire or nurture the younger team. Some didn't even try. They'd clock in, get the job done, and clock out, with little thought for the bigger picture.

Meanwhile, some of the youngest and least experienced members of the team...the apprentices, the ones fresh out of school...were the most natural leaders. They were enthusiastic, eager to learn, and genuinely wanted to be a part of something bigger. They just got it. They understood the culture we were trying to build. The way they treated each other, spoke with clients, and let their actions speak louder than words.

Even back then, I knew it. I could see the kids were the future of the business. But what could I do? You can't put a first-year apprentice in charge of a job site...it's not fair on them or the client. At the same time, I hated the idea of someone representing the company who didn't align with our values. It was a constant balancing act: trying to grow the business while staying true to what we believed in.

Looking back, I know I was in a bit of a holding pattern. It was so important to maintain the high standards we were aiming for, and that meant I had to rely on the experienced ones for quality. But deep down, I was investing everything into the younger crew. They were the ones I spent the most time with, the ones I earmarked as future leaders.

At times, it felt like an impossible trade-off...quality or culture...pick one. In the early years, it seemed like you couldn't have both. Always robbing Peter to pay Paul. But I couldn't accept that. I focused on training and mentoring the younger team members, pouring as much time and energy into them as I could. I wanted them to have the tools not just to do the job, but to lead...to embody the culture we were trying to build.

It wasn't easy. The young ones had so much potential, but they lacked technical experience, and the experienced ones didn't align with the culture. It was frustrating, but I reminded myself that leadership isn't just about years of experience. You can still be a leader on your first day...through your attitude, your actions, and the way you treat others. That's what kept me going. I saw glimmers in those apprentices, and I knew if we were patient, we'd eventually have both: quality and culture.

Now, looking back at where we've come, I can confidently say that patience has paid off. Those kids I invested in are now running jobs, leading teams, and representing our business in a way I'm proud of. The magic happens when you mix quality and culture. It's when your best leaders are in the right positions, bringing out the best in everyone around them.

The biggest lesson? Growth isn't about how fast you can move or how many people you can hire. It's about building something sustainable. It's about sticking to your values, even when it feels like the harder road. And most importantly, it's about putting your energy into the right people...the ones who'll take your business where you want to go.

And at the heart of it all is the simplicity of *'don't be a dickhead'*. It's a moral compass...a pub test for behaviour. If someone starts venturing into that territory, it doesn't mean they're a bad person, but it does mean they need a reality check. Calling it out, "Hey, you're being a bit of a dickhead," becomes the system for accountability.

We had one girl early on who kept dipping into poor behaviour. It wasn't outright horrible, but it didn't pass the pub test. People around her got sick of it and called her out. Eventually, she left on her own accord. That was the system working. It doesn't mean she was a bad person; she just wasn't aligned with what we were building. And that's okay. Not everyone fits, and that's why values matter.

In the end, the *'don't be a dickhead'* rule isn't just about avoiding bad behaviour; it's about building a culture where everyone holds each other accountable and works toward something bigger than themselves.

Don't Be a Dickhead

The prison gig started like most jobs do: with a promising opportunity and a sense of adventure. We'd been picking up more and more maintenance painting work, and by then, we'd painted just about everything you could imagine...retirement homes, council buildings, theme parks, even those colourful huts on Brighton Beach. But nothing had quite prepared us for what was waiting behind the gates of Marngoneet Correctional Centre.

Before we get to that madness, let me tell you about Adventure Park in Geelong. That job was the highlight of our maintenance work. Every spring, before the park reopened for the season, we'd roll in to freshen things up. It was like walking into a giant playground for grown-ups...mini-golf course, archery targets, water slides. Not exactly your average day of painting.

That park was a whole different world...bright, bustling and ambitious. The entire place was set around a stunning lake, its still waters reflecting the towering water slides and colourful rides. The air was alive with the chatter of ducks and birds mingling with the distant hum of power tools and the occasional laugh of a tradie. Perfectly manicured lawns and gardens bordered every path, and even in its unfinished state, the park was always picturesque.

Every spring, it was the same routine: a mad rush of tradies scrambling to get things finished just in time for opening day. You'd think with the park only operating for half the year, there'd be plenty of time to prepare, but no. Without fail, they'd dream up something ambitious...like a brand-new ride or a big new building for change rooms...three weeks out from the gates reopening. And there'd we'd be, racing the clock with painters, carpenters, landscapers, and electricians all bumping into one another, trying to hit impossible deadlines.

For us, it was always part of the fun. The transformation from tradie chaos to theme park chaos was something to behold. One minute, the air was thick with the smell of sawdust and fresh paint. The next, it was the sugary scent of fairy floss, hot chips, and the delighted squeals of kids riding the freshly tested roller coasters.

We were often still painting when the first visitors rolled in, hurriedly touching up the handrails or adding the final coats to the mini-golf obstacles. But it all somehow came together at the last minute, year after year. Seeing the park come to life...bright colours, Ferris wheels, and families pouring through the gates with wide-eyed excitement, made the frantic lead up worth it.

I'll never forget the year they were installing this brand new multi-million-dollar twin water slide. It was a beast, twisting and looping like a rollercoaster on steroids. The owners were buzzing about it, and rightly so. They even flew in a couple of Canadian water slide engineers to test the thing. Now, these guys had the dream job...travelling the world to ride water slides. When the owner introduced them, he said, "They're such great guys". Of course they were! You'd be in a pretty great mood too if your job was basically a never-ending summer vacation. Their task? Go down the slide a hundred times to measure water flow, speed, and some other nonsense that probably didn't matter but sounded important. They knocked it out with smiles on their faces, and for the next hundred runs, they needed volunteers. That's when the painters on-site dropped their brushes, threw on their bathers, and lined up like kids at recess giving their 'feedback' to the water engineers (happy Canadian Pro Water Sliders).

That's the kind of work we loved...fun, unique, and full of stories to tell. But then came the prison gig...a charming little facility filled with society's finest.

At first, it seemed like a straightforward job. Paint some walls, spruce up the handrails and keep the warden happy. But a prison is no theme park, and the stakes were a little higher than freshening up a mini-golf course.

The prison yard was nothing like I'd imagined. Maybe I'd been influenced by too many movies, expecting bench seats scattered around a grimy rectangle like *Shawshank Redemption,* or brawls breaking out left, right and centre like in *Prison Break.* I half expected to see loved ones pressing their hands against glass partitions, exchanging tearful goodbyes. But what we walked into was... shockingly casual.

This was a low-security prison, sure, but it felt more like a budget university campus than anything out of Hollywood. The grounds were open and spacious. Inmates wandered freely in groups, laughing and chatting like they were between lectures rather than serving time. *The fashion was all very similar.* A game of basketball was in full swing...did I see they had a pool?

I sent one of the younger guys to start the job. He was a skinny, curly-haired guy that had not long ago finished his apprenticeship. He had a cheeky streak that inmates loved. They told him that he'd get blown away by the wind and called him Noodles. We were never sure if they were teasing his curly hair or skinny build. But he had a knack for getting along with everyone...even the guys behind the bars. He'd eat lunch with them, trading barbs like he'd known them for years and raving about the chicken schnitzel rolls they served.

But things took a turn. Midway through a perfectly ordinary day of scraping and rolling, one of the prisoners struck up a conversation. They talked about work, the painting, life in general...small talk, you know. Then Noodles, in his infinite naivety, asked the one question you never ask in prison. "What are you in here for?"

The prisoner didn't miss a beat. "I killed the last painter who worked here," he said casually, like he was ordering a coffee.

That wasn't even the worst of it. Strict tool counts were mandatory, and every item had to be accounted for at the end of the day. One afternoon, the putty knife came up missing. Now, a putty knife in the hands of a painter is harmless enough...good for scraping paint, opening paint tins, glazing windows or even flipping your toasted sandwich. But in the hands of a prisoner? That's a whole different toolkit.

Cue the lockdown. Sirens wailed. Guards stormed in like it was a SWAT raid. Every inch of the prison was searched, every shadow combed through. Inmates were caught between two moods: some were clearly thrilled by the action and some annoyed that their basketball game or card session had been rudely interrupted. Our guy...sweating bullets in the corner of the yard, fiddling with his paint roller, imagining his rogue putty knife started a prison riot. He could practically see his face on the front page of the local paper under the headline, *"Painter's Tool Sparks Prison Riot!"*

And me? I had no idea this was happening. Phones weren't allowed in the prison, so I was blissfully unaware of the chaos unfolding. For all I knew he was still rolling a fresh coat of paint. Hours dragged on, each one probably feeling like a year to him. Finally, the search came to an anticlimactic end. The knife was found, lying harmlessly in a garden bed. It had fallen off his scissor lift, not into the hands of an inmate with a grudge. Crisis averted. But relief was short lived... he got a dressing down from the guards so intense, you'd think he'd personally handed the prisoners a hacksaw and blueprint of the place.

By the time he finally made it out of there, he looked like he'd aged about five years. He called me, his voice a mix of nerves and exhaustion, recounting every painful detail. It was the kind of chaos you couldn't script if you tried, but hey, at least no one managed to start a riot with a rogue putty knife. Crisis averted...for now.

Another episode in this sitcom came a week later. I got a call, and it was Noodles, rattled and desperate.

"I can't do it anymore," he blurted out, his words filled with panic. "I can't do the painting. The handrails... they can't be painted."

I stifle a laugh and try to sound serious. "What's happened now?"

He took a deep breath, "I'm painting the handrails, right? Doing my thing. But there's this one prisoner...this one muppet...that keeps scratching the paint off with his fingernails as soon as I'm done. I've painted the same handrail six fucking times!"

At this point I'm trying not to lose it. "So, what, he's just standing there, waiting for you to finish each coat?"

"Exactly!" Noodles cried. "He's lurking and then when I leave, clawing at it like a feral cat!"

And then Noodles added, his voice sounded fed up, not quite yet seeing the funny side. "He's the same guy I was telling you about last week," he continues. "Same fucking guy...buggy guy."

Oh yes, buggy guy. The infamous prisoner who'd already earned his reputation with Noodles the previous week. Noodles had been tasked with driving one of those little golf buggies around the prison to carry all his gear, and this guy had made it his life's work to troll him.

Apparently Buggy Guy had a brilliant strategy: he would walk as slow as humanly possible directly in front of the buggy, forcing Noodles to crawl along at a snail's pace.

"The man's a menace!"

Now I could've given him a speech about resilience, about sticking it out, but the image of some menace clawing the fresh paint off handrails like it was his full-time job broke me. I laughed again, gave him a break, and started a rotating system. New workers would cycle in, paint for a week or two, and come back with their own war stories and full stomachs from those prison schnitzels.

The prison job became legend...a bizarre chapter in our company's history, retold at every Christmas party. And while it didn't directly tie into the 'don't be a dickhead' ethos, it taught us a thing or two about patience, adaptability...no it didn't. It was just a great story I wanted to wedge in.

It does remind you of the weird and wonderful places this business would take us. Sometimes, you've just got to roll with the chaos, laugh it off, and hope the next job has fewer lockdowns and better lunch options.

CHAPTER 3

NEGOTIATING

Negotiation and I have never been best mates. In fact, for most of my life, I've been a shocking negotiator. If there's a skill involved in haggling, I was born without it. Take, for instance, the time I went to the Grand Bazaar in Turkey. This place is haggler's paradise...a sprawling maze of stalls filled with spices, carpet, jewellery, and vendors who could sell sand to a camel. Everyone brags about walking away with these incredible bargains. Me? I walked out having paid full price for a tea set I didn't even want. I've got countless stories like that. Once in Mexico, I foolishly decided to take charge of the haggling...rookie mistake. It was for a simple transfer to the airport, something even a mildly competent negotiator could manage. The mere memory of it makes me want to crawl under the nearest table. I can barely bring myself to share the details but let me paint a quick picture: we ended up nowhere near the airport, paid triple the going rate, and, just to top it all off, got our credit card skimmed. A true masterclass in negotiating.

I'm not cut out for jobs where negotiation is a core skill. A real estate agent? Forget it...I'd probably sell someone a house and throw in a car to close the deal. Hostage negotiator? Let's not even go there...I'd probably end up trading myself.

But running a business changes things. Suddenly, you're thrown into a world where negotiation isn't optional...it's survival. And trust me, I learned the hard way. Clients can be cagey, trying to squeeze every freebie out of you. Workers are always looking to negotiate their pays, perks, and sometimes their work hours. You'd think running a business would turn you into some master dealmaker, but in my case, it felt more like being dropped into a never-ending game of Monopoly where I wanted everyone to own a few hotels and streets.

Even my young nieces taught me a thing or two about negotiating. I've lost my fair share of negotiations with the girls aged from two-four. In fact, *have I ever won one*? They've got that relentless energy where they won't back down until they've worn you out. I started to learn to hold your ground, or they'll end up running the show. *Who am I kidding? They still run the show.* But at least these days, I'm wheeling and dealing with them. "You want a lollipop?" *Sure, mate. But you're taking the bins out first.* All about finding that win-win.

The thing is, I had to get better at it. Negotiation isn't just about saving money or getting a deal...it's about setting boundaries, protecting your time, and making sure your team and clients respect what you're building. If you don't learn to negotiate, you'll end up overworked, undervalued, and probably out of business.

In negotiation, the way you handle disagreements is key to maintaining an open, productive dialogue. Never outright disagree with the other party. When someone feels challenged or undermined, they tend to dig in their heels and become defensive, which can shut down any hope of collaboration. Instead, focus on finding a common belief or shared goal. Even if your views differ, highlighting areas of agreement keeps the conversation constructive and opens the door to a solution.

One of the most important principles is to show you're negotiating in good faith. This means being transparent, authentic, and truly interested in finding a solution that works for both sides. Understanding the other party's needs, concerns, and motivations is crucial to crafting a solution that feels fair. Show empathy and curiosity about their perspective...it helps foster trust and signals that you're willing to compromise.

Equally important is managing emotions. Negative emotions like frustration or distrust can derail a negotiation. Your goal should be to de-escalate tension and build rapport. By amplifying positive emotions...optimism, trust, shared interest...you increase the chances of a successful outcome. It's about creating an environment where both parties feel heard and respected, which in turn opens the path to finding a workable solution.

So, while I still wouldn't trust myself in a Turkish market or selling a house, I've come a long way. Negotiation might not come naturally to me, but it's like any other skill...you just must learn, adapt, and maybe start with something small...like trading lollipops for taking the bins out.

A Cautionary Tale

Let me tell you a story about how not to handle a negotiation. Picture this: I was dealing with a builder we'd worked with for over five years. Solid relationship overall, but we were barely scraping by on their jobs. On this one project, they'd changed the scope so much that I was sure we deserved some extras to be paid. I'd been meaning to call the director to discuss what was fair...I had all the extras and original scope written down, so I was ready to negotiate.

Anyway, on this day I'm walking down Smith Street in Collingwood. Everyone seemed to be dressed the same... the men in dark blue, black and grey...browns a bit iffy. Not a suit in sight. Plenty of second-hand, vintage, or reworked garments sourced from thrift stores. Flannel shirts, denim jackets, and high-waisted jeans are staples.

With a sensory overload of hipster culture, I walked way too close to a Tesla and set off its alarm. The wide sidewalks offer a clear path...but don't get too comfortable. Between the endless sprawl of outdoor dining spots and groups strolling three-wide, navigating the street becomes an obstacle course. And, if you're lucky, you might bump into one of Collingwood's iconic local characters. There's Carrot Man, a legend in his own right, parading a two-metre papier-mâché carrot like it's the most normal thing in the world. Or, *The Bike Man*, who whizzes by on the walkway, towing a collection of anywhere between six to fifteen carriages...sometimes a mix of stolen bikes, prams, or whatever other vessel he's acquired that week. No wonder I walked into a Tesla and set off an alarm...it's all part of the local experience!

That's when my phone starts buzzing...it's the director. Just seeing his name throws me into a mood. He's a decent guy, but this job has me on edge, and I'm convinced we haven't been looked after. So, with all that brewing, I answer. I've got my laptop in the office with all the extras listed on a spreadsheet, and my negotiating notes...but I'm running purely on frustration. I don't want to sit on it any longer, and instead of staying calm, I dive into attack mode. The car alarm is still blaring, and I'm losing my thought process left and right.

"Hey," I say, my tone already flat.

"Hi," he replies, not sounding combative, nor in the mood for small talk. "I thought I'd give you a quick call about your invoice query. I want to go over the extras you've submitted."

"Oh, good," I snap, jumping in before he can continue. "Because honestly, this is getting ridiculous. You keep changing the scope.

NEGOTIATING

We've gone through 25 different colours, for crying out loud. That's not what we agreed on!"

There's a slight pause, just long enough to make me feel like I went a bit hard.

"Well," he starts, his voice calm and deliberate, "your terms and conditions don't specify a limit on the number of colours. So, technically..."

"Technically?" I cut him off, the frustration in my voice impossible to hide. "I'm going off the original scope which didn't have us painting a fucking rainbow."

He doesn't engage in combat, "I understand your frustration," he says smoothly. "But unless there's something specific in writing about a cap in colours or types of paint, we're within the agreed terms."

It's at this point I realise I need my notes. I'd written down something about how I hoped given our strong relationship we could work together on this...I'd had dates of an email confirming some colours...not this many? My brain is struggling to keep up. *Is that Tesla alarm getting louder?*

"Look," I say, fumbling to make my point. "We've spent hours... days even, just sourcing these paint colours, let alone the time it's taken to continue to pack up and start with a new colour. Surely you can see that?"

"Sure," he replies, still maddingly composed. "But the scope does say, on page seventy-one, the painter is to handle painting to specification, and the specification allows for variation in colours."

My blood pressure is skyrocketing, "Variation? This is the whole fucking Dulux catalogue."

I can practically hear him smiling on the other end. "I can understand your position," he says, his voice still even. "But we must stick to the agreement. Unless you can point to something in the contract that specifies otherwise..."

"Point to something in the contract?" I interrupt. But there's no need to continue. We're going around in circles and I've lost my head. I'm not making sense anymore. Without my notes, I'm all over the place, forgetting key points and repeating myself. The car alarm is still going off, and my focus has slipped completely.

"Alright," he says finally, his tone suggesting he's ready to wrap things up. "If you'd like to provide any additional documentation or specific points for us to review, feel free to send them through. For now, though, I think we've covered the main points."

I hung up, fuming, stuck my finger up to the phone. Long story short, I didn't get the extras paid that I thought we deserved. Worse yet, I probably strained what had been a good relationship. I still think he could have been more human, less robot given our relationship. But that's not the point I'm trying to make. I'd gone in all guns blazing without a proper plan. I ended up sounding like a man arguing with a brick wall while a car alarm provided the soundtrack.

By the time the job wrapped up, my only thought was, thankfully, that it's over. I didn't feel the normal pride I'd have handing over a job. The lesson hit hard: don't negotiate when you're in an emotional headspace or out of a controlled environment. At least I was in Smith Street...my favourite place in the world. I went and had a beer at *The Grace Darling*, and things were good again.

A Negotiation Victory

Ah yes...the time I didn't blow it.

A passive-aggressive email rolls in. You know the type...as per my last email blah blah, for future reference blah blah, if you could get back to me at your earliest convenience, thanks in advance for your prompt response. And of course, his cohort that he would have been bitching about us to, has been cc'd in on the action.

The email is full of accusations, here we go, veiled threats, and more condensation than I thought was possible. The builder was convinced we hadn't finished the job we said we would, despite me having the receipts, literally, to prove him wrong. We were only told to paint the new and not touch the existing. My quote said exactly that. Their director and his foreman weren't on the same page. Nothing to do with me. I knew he was out of line. He, of course, disagreed, and his email basically screamed, let's fight.

It fired me up, but did I get straight on the phone to fire off an emotional response? This time, I went to have a coffee instead.

The moment I stepped into the cafe, I was hit by that rich, unmistakable aroma of freshly roasted beans...Coffee Supreme beans, no less. This wasn't your run of the mill brew... it was the real deal. The kind of coffee that makes you appreciate why people obsess over coffee in Melbourne. This isn't the story of a big negotiation, but I did recently have a spirited debate about Melbourne coffee. A friend from outside of Melbourne tried to downplay the reputation, saying, "You can get coffee that good anywhere". Now, anyone who's spent time sipping Melbourne brews knows this isn't just about quality...it's about consistency. I made my case, explaining that it's not a question of finding good coffee here and there; in Melbourne, it's rare to find a bad one. Every cup is pretty much guaranteed to hit the spot.

Small victory on that front...but not quite the negotiation tale I'm getting to. I digress.

The cabinets were packed with temptation: blueberry muffins that looked like they belonged in a glossy magazine, strawberry tarts that shimmered under the lights, and homemade cake that had me debating whether to order just one slice or the whole cake.

If it was a weekend, the place would be packed. A forty-minute wait for a table, courtesy of being featured in an article by Urban List. The second that two or more people know about a spot in Collingwood, its hipster status is done. But let me tell you, they still have the best sandwiches in Melbourne. And that's saying something, because there are more sandwich shops here than actual people. It's become something of a sandwich cult. Honestly, if there's a cult worth joining, it's one fuelled by great coffee and the best sandwiches in Collingwood...I'm all in.

But let's be honest: this isn't a story about coffee and sandwiches. It was about procrastination. Just like the procrastinating that's happening right now on telling the actual story. I'd stepped in to the cafe to blow off steam, but really, I was blowing off responsibility. The muffins, the tarts, the cults, and revisiting debates about coffee...they were all distractions. Eventually, I drained the last sip of coffee and knew what I had to do. The cafe had done its job...it had given me space to think. But now it was time to face the music.

Coffee under my belt, I stationed myself in a quiet spot in the office and prepared. The four P's...Preparation Prevents Poor Performance. I wasn't going in under-prepared this time. I rang our supervisor and double-checked every detail of the job. Armed myself with all the facts and our original quote and the email trail. I took my time and prepared for battle... calmly.

When I finally called him back, he didn't waste any time...he came out like a boxer in the first round.

"I've had it! That job's not finished, and I don't care what your quote says!" he shouted, his voice escalating with every word.

I took a deep breath and tried keeping my tone even. "Alright, let's take it from the top. What exactly are we talking about here?"

"You didn't paint the existing part of the property! The job needed to be done weeks ago, and the client's pissed off."

"Right," I said, glancing at my notes. "You're referring to the existing part of the house we were told by your foreman when I quoted not to touch? The one excluded in your quote? Page two, second item?" *Maybe that last bit came out a bit sassy.*

There was a pause on his end, followed by a muttered, "Fuck this and fuck that".

I pressed on, still measured. "Look, I get you're frustrated if you thought we were painting the entire project for that price, in that deadline. But I can send the email trail with your project coordinator on the 3rd of March at 10:11am and it clearly says just to allow for the new part of the house. I've also got a screenshot I'm sending though now of your guy confirming that we will be done with the new part by the deadline, and they'll let me know if the existing needs quoting."

This is getting met with some huffing and puffing, and muttering something along the lines of, "My foreman is also a fuckwit".

"Put yourself in my shoes," that one's a real favourite of mine. "I got told to do the new part of the house, have confirmed it multiple times via quote, contract, email and text. And I've done what I've been asked and now you're abusing me."

"I'm not abusing you," he starts to concede. "This entire project has been chaos. The client is not happy with me, it's just been one thing after another. You can't imagine!"

"I can imagine," I hit back, but quickly steadied. "It's a bit to manage. But taking it out on the painters who did exactly what they were hired to do isn't going to fix it," trying my best to sound empathetic but not wavering.

Another pause. Then like a balloon losing air, "It's all good, I'm not blaming you. Miscommunication on our end. I'll sort it out."

I still stuck my finger up at the phone as I hung up, but this time with a lot more satisfaction than frustration.

Lesson learned: there's real power in pausing, prepping, being in the right environment and staying cool under pressure. And the other lesson. Sometimes, you've got to stop debating coffee, put down the sandwiches, and pick up the phone.

Anyway, back to *The Grace Darling* for a pint of Stone + Wood... things are good again.

CHAPTER 4

NEVER MISS TWICE

The concept of 'never miss twice' is all about resilience and self-awareness. It's about getting back on track...quickly. It's not about striving for perfection, but breaking cycles of bad habits before they snowball into something bigger. Life, fitness, work, or even personal growth...it's a mindset.

Take a simple example: you've had a few beers on a Friday night (standard), and by Saturday you've hit up Maccas and spent the day watching cricket on the couch. We've all been there. But the difference between a bad day and a bad week is what you choose to do next. Snap out of it. Go for a walk, lace up for a quick jog. Or maybe at least walk to Maccas. Depending on how many beers you've had, maybe going in, instead of the drive-through might be all you're capable of. These small actions don't just break the cycle...they set the tone for the next day. Compare that to the time you let it slide...Saturday rolls into Sunday, and before you know it, you're in a rut. The longer you wait, the harder it gets.

It's the same with teaching skills or behaviour. Mistakes happen, and they're nothing to beat yourself up over. This whole book is basically about mistakes. But repeating the mistakes isn't just an oversight...it's the foundation of a bad habit. Let's say someone forgets their drop sheet while painting. Once is an accident. Twice is a pattern. By the third or fourth time, it's a full-blown habit, and you're dealing with overspray or spilled paint and unnecessary work. The better workers knock it on the head themselves, and you don't even need to intervene. But for others, you'll need to address it straight away...don't let it become their habit.

Take health as another example. Maybe you have a can of coke on a Sunday night...that's fine. But what happens on Monday when you reach for another? Before you know it, there's a coke next to your plate every night at dinner, and it's no longer a treat...it's a routine. On the other hand, if you drink more water on a Monday, you feel better, and suddenly Coke is just an occasional treat again. *Anyway, when did I venture into giving health advice?*

It's the mindset I'm trying to articulate. If you get burned by a bad contractor, that can happen. If you go back to them for another job and get burned again, that's on you. The same goes for clients who constantly change scope but refuse to pay any extras...if you let it slide once, they'll keep pushing boundaries.

The 'never miss twice' principle isn't about avoiding mistakes altogether...that's impossible. It's about minimising their impact and preventing them from becoming a habit. Whether it's your diet, your fitness routine, or how you train apprentices or run your business, the lesson is clear: don't dwell on them, learn from each stumble, move forward, and stay consistent.

Unexplained Mysteries

It started with promise...a subcontractor who could wield a spray gun like an artist. Quick, efficient, and capable of smashing out ceilings and undercoats faster than most. He was an asset on the right job. But there was baggage, and it was impossible to miss.

When he first showed up on-site, he looked like a grub, paint and fillers plastered all over his pants and T-shirt. His boots were falling apart. Drop sheets? An optional luxury. Overspray? Well, he treated it like his personal signature.

Still, I was in a phase of focusing on what people could do. I was backing people in, maybe a little too much. That was easier than having a tough conversation, right? "He's fast, he's good with a spray gun," I'd reason with myself. So, instead, I worked around it. I'd send him to spray ceilings and undercoats, jobs that he couldn't make a mess of, and our better painters could follow to tidy up.

For a while, this plan worked. He'd breeze through jobs, leaving ceilings and walls perfectly primed. But then we needed him on a higher-stakes project... a new house where the kitchen and floorboards were already installed. I should've seen it coming.

"Got the kitchen and living room areas finished," he'd tell me, wiping paint from his hands to his beard, "a day ahead of schedule." He wasn't wrong. But I walked in, and my stomach sank. Paint flecks dotted the floorboards and cabinets like a bad case of chickenpox. Two days of cleaning up later, the kitchen sparkled again. We'd got it cleaned up before anyone had seen it. But the damage to efficiency and my patience...was done.

I pulled him aside. "Mate, you've got to be more careful masking up, using drop sheets, take care of the space." He nodded seriously. "Got it, won't happen again." But I'd seen enough to know it's hard to change the spots on an old leopard.

A month later, it happened again. He skipped masking on some built-in robes, and the client did walk in this time, only to find paint freckles across their brand-new messmate joinery. "What's this?" they snapped, pointing at the overspray. The culprit wasn't too hard to find...the bloke with paint through his hair and maybe in his ears...because my message hadn't got through!

Another conversation. This time firmer. "You've got to slow down, mask up. Drop sheets, no excuses!" He nodded again, eyes at his festy shoes. "I'll do better."

A few weeks later, I caught him painting a window without a drop sheet. No spills yet, but waiting for disaster. "Final warning!" I told him. "I'll just go get a drop sheet," he fired back, as if it was isolated and I was out of line. I reminded my supervisors to not let it slide. Do as I say not as I do and all that, because I was more guilty than them for letting this slide.

The last straw came when the client rang, furious. "Your painter... the messy one...was up on a ladder on my freshly varnished floorboards. No drop sheets." There was no tangible damage this time, just damage to our reputation.

That was it. I had to move him on. It wasn't about the ladder on the floorboards...it was about the pattern and the refusal to change. Looking back, the red flags were there from the start. That's the problem with experience sometimes, they can be experienced at the wrong thing. And it's hard to change.

Months later, I heard he was still telling people, "The fuckhead sacked me for having a ladder on the floorboards". Not true, of course. He missed twice, three, four times. It's not about one mistake. It's about what you do after the first one.

Anyway, not every story about painters and their antics ends on such a sour note. Let me tell you about another situation, one that still makes me laugh when think about it. This one's less about drop sheets and overspray, and more about a simple, honest mistake that turned into one of the most bizarre days of my career. And don't worry...I'll stay on track this time.

It was one of those scorching days where the sun was out to fry anyone daring enough to work outdoors, and the air was thick enough to make you question every life decision. I was drowning in paperwork...just the usual soul-sucking kind...when my phone buzzed. It was one of our painters, a solid worker, but let's just say he wasn't exactly firing or all cylinders that day.

He was in Lorne that hot day to oil a deck. Simple enough, right? The builder had washed it and cleared it the day before, so all we had to do was oil it twice in one day, and it would be good to go...until next summer, of course. I thought this phone call can't come with too many curveballs...as simple as a job can get. I'd even ordered the oil and had organised all his equipment. All he had to do was pick it up at the warehouse and do the application.

He starts with the oddball question, "Should we move the furniture before painting?"

Now, I'm sitting here thinking, when did we become an interior design firm? But, hey, I keep it cool, answer him, and try get back to the mountain of paperwork in front of me. Maybe the builder forgot to take off the furniture?

The day progresses with the normal peaks and troughs...but nothing more from our man in Lorne. He must have managed to get the pot plant or barbecue or whatever was on the deck out of his way. The day was getting close to the end...so he must be almost done. He calls back, "Should I paint the bench seats too?"

Wait, what bench seats? My brain does a quick scramble. That's when it all clicked...he was at the wrong house. Painting a completely different deck. For a completely different person. Someone who had probably no idea their backyard was in the middle of getting a free facelift.

I couldn't help but laugh at the absurdity of it. But now we had a situation. So, we did what any self-respecting painter would do... and in the grand tradition of owning up to a monumental stuff-up, we left a polite note on the freshly painted deck. Something like, "Surprise! Your deck's on us today!" Then, like stealthy ninjas, we vanished without a trace. The reason this whole mix up had happened was that our painter had done a quick scan of the job board and spec, and the address on our app, but instead of double-checking, he pulled into the house next door. He'd misread the number. Now, this isn't the best example of never missing twice. It's more of a fair stuff up that could have turned out worse. After all, who doesn't appreciate a fresh, free oil on their deck?

The silver lining is that he's never done it again, I mean, let's be real; you should never miss like that, even once! But hey, at least it made for a funny story we can all laugh about now. And while it wasn't exactly a model moment of learning, it certainly kept the day interesting.

We never heard a peep from the homeowners. To this day, I wonder if they came home and stared at their newly painted deck, thinking, "Did we somehow forgot we hired a painter?" Or maybe they just shrugged, figured they'd won the home improvement lottery, and cracked open a cold one. Either way, they got a free paint job, and we got one hell of a story for the ages.

So, what's the takeaway from these two tales? Well, the first guy... everyone makes mistakes, but if you can't right a wrong, if you're too set in your bad habits, you end up painting yourself into a corner...pun intended!

Then there's the other guy, who didn't miss the mark...he missed the entire house. One big, stupid mistake. But here's the thing: he owned it and made sure never to make that mistake again. And later, laughed about it. It's proof that your response to failure is everything.

At the end of the day, mistakes are inevitable. Some are small and sneaky, like overspray on a cupboard. Others are loud and ridiculous, like painting the wrong house. The lessons stay the same: own your mess, learn from it, and don't miss twice.

CHAPTER 5

EXECUTION OVER OUTCOME

Business, like life, comes with no guarantees. You can plan, analyse, and strategise all you want, but the outcome? That's never fully in your control. What is in your control is how you execute... your standards, your processes, your ability to adapt and deliver regardless of external forces.

A job can get thrown off course in a hundred ways...unexpected weather, last-minute client changes, a competitor slashing their price to undercut you. In those moments, you either react emotionally, chasing an outcome you can't control, or you double down on execution. Because that's the only constant.

Look at the Richmond Football Club. They built their dynasty by mastering this principle...focusing on execution over outcome. Injuries? Bad umpiring? A freakish performance from an opposition player like, the Bont? All part of the game. You can't control any of it. But what Richmond did better than anyone during their premiership years was stick to their system, no matter what. They didn't let setbacks shake their identity.

Emma Murray, their mindfulness coach, captured it perfectly: *"Focus on the controllables"*. It's not just a sporting philosophy; it's a blueprint for business, for leadership, for life. Richmond didn't win by chasing results. They won by executing their processes, repeatedly, trusting that the results would follow.

It's the same for us. Every project, every conversation, every job... our responsibility is to execute our values. Do things the right way, even when it's hard. Even when it doesn't seem like it's paying off. Because when you commit to execution, not just outcomes, the long game starts working in your favour.

That's what this book has become for me...a reference point. A *'what would I do'* manual for when things inevitably go sideways. The answer is always the same: stick to the values, execute to the highest standard, and let the outcome take care of itself. That's the game.

A Big Tall American Kicking Goals in Speed Dealers

It was the early days...chaotic, raw, and full of dangerous optimism. We were just beginning to sink our claws into the commercial scene in Melbourne, chasing big projects and even bigger dreams. One day, the phone rang with an opportunity too tempting to resist: a sprawling office space in Richmond for a new and exciting commercial builder. This was exactly the kind of project we dreamed of...a challenging, high-profile job that could catapult us with a builder who seemed to align perfectly with us. Their pipeline of work was impressive, full of exciting, innovative projects around Melbourne's most exciting suburbs. They needed us to sharpen our price, razor sharp. It was a calculated risk worth taking. Balance was key here...this wasn't about recklessness but rather an informed gamble on the type of opportunity that could transform the trajectory of Paint It Black.

We went all in, lattes in hard from Top Paddock and Pillar of Salt...$5 shots of optimism fuelling the team. The project had everything we could hope for: complexity, excitement, and a chance to prove ourselves. The site manager was a gem, a rare breed who understood the delicate balance between chaos and camaraderie. Fridays meant beers at Harlow, a ritual that kept morale high and the paint flowing. Parking fines would soon become a line item in the budget, and I tipped my life savings into smashed avos and caffeine. This wasn't just work...it was an adventure, and a peculiar type of madness.

The job itself was a beauty: complex, challenging, and with just enough chaos to keep the adrenaline spiked. Panel timber ceilings loomed above like wooden cathedrals, demanding the kind of precision that can drive a painter insane. The crew loved it. They thrived on the rhythm of the work and the energy of the project. This was the Melbourne dream in its purest form.

As the final strokes of paint dried, the numbers started to haunt me. The hours had evaporated faster than summer rain on asphalt, and profit felt like a distant memory. It was tempting...so tempting...to cut corners, to speed things up, to just get it done and call it a day. But here's the thing: cutting corners would've only compounded the loss. Sure, we might have salvaged a fraction of the time, but at what cost? A rushed job would've turned the builder sour, and not only would we have lost profit on this job, but we'd have also blown any chance of future work with them. That's the kind of ripple effect you can't afford.

So, as we were in Richmond, we took a leaf out of the premiership-winning Richmond Tigers' playbook. We doubled down on execution. Sometimes, a seven-foot American kicks a bag of goals on you while rocking speed dealers, and you must take the loss (Collingwood and Richmond supporters will feel that one). But here's the point: you don't let that big American...or any setback, for that matter...shake your values or change who you are. It tests you, no doubt. You'll feel the pressure to waver, to compromise, to do something that isn't you. But when you stick fat, when you hold firm to your identity, the results will come.

For us, that meant leaning into the standards we had promised in our tender submission. We were committed to delivering a high-quality job that we'd be proud of, no matter what the numbers looked like. Sure, Paint It Black weren't going to win the next two grand finals off the back of this one, but if we executed well here, we could win the next few jobs with this builder. This was a test of execution over outcome. The outcome wasn't what we wanted... there was no sugarcoating that, but we couldn't change it now. What we could control was how we responded.

So, we finished strong. Every detail was nailed. Every touch-up, every coat, every interaction with the builder reflected the standards we hold ourselves to. And when the dust settled, the builder was thrilled, the client was thrilled, and the crew walked away proud. That's the thing about execution...it's not just about the job at hand. It's about building trust, reputation, and opportunities. This job might've left us in the red, but it put us firmly in the black when it came to relationships and future work.

But pride doesn't pay the bills. The end of job review felt like a postmortem. What had gone wrong? What could we learn?

The answer was clear...those damn panel ceilings. Each room had beams strategically placed, not for architectural beauty, but seemingly to wage psychological warfare on our mobile scaffold set up. Every few metres, the scaffold had to be dismantled and rebuilt, a labour-intensive task that bled hours. Polished plaster walls added another layer of cruelty...spraying was out of the question.

The scaffold logistics had turned into a time sink we hadn't fully anticipated. Lesson learned. We reviewed, refined, and adjusted our quoting process, ensuring we factor in this new detail.

In hindsight, that project was the foundation of a relationship that turned into a game-changer for us. The builder became one of our most fruitful clients, bringing us incredible projects across Melbourne's best suburbs. The risk had paid off, but it also came with a cautionary note: these jobs in fancy suburbs look great on the socials, but they're not always where the real profit lies. It can be the mundane maintenance work on shopping centres in Sunshine...the unsexy jobs, that keep the lights on. We learned to balance both. Exploit the profitable side of your business to fund the aspirational ones.

In the end, this job was worth the initial hit. It taught us that sometimes you must play the long game, investing in relationships and opportunities that align with your vision. And when you stay true to your values, execute to the best of your abilities, and learn from every challenge, the results, financial and otherwise...will take care of themselves (unless you run into a big American kicking goals in speed dealers).

CHAPTER 6

BUTTFACE MEETINGS

It's crucial to strike the balance between taking your work seriously and not taking yourself too seriously. This mindset keeps you grounded, humble and open to growth. In the book *Good to Great* by Jim Collins, there's a clear correlation between CEOs with little to no ego and the success of their companies. These leaders are often described as plough horses and not show horses...focused on the hard work and the success of their team rather than personal glory. The best CEOs constantly emphasise how lucky they are to have their teams, showcasing their humility. Meanwhile, ego-driven leaders, who make it all about themselves, often achieve far less sustained success.

Zoe Foster-Blake spoke about how she refers to luck as a dirty word because she was constantly talking about how much luck she had...whether it was having a great executive team or being surrounded by talented advisors. She would emphasise how lucky she felt to have such good people supporting her. However, over time, she learned to take pride in her hard work and to say, *"I've done a hard thing, and I should be proud of it"*.

What struck me during her talk was the balance she'd found between humility and confidence. Even while she's now more open about being proud of her achievements, Zoe still often credits the people around her and recognises how lucky she's been to have great support. This speaks to a larger trend among successful leaders who stay humble and ego-free, acknowledging their team's role in their success...something seen in leaders who build sustainable success through teamwork, not just individual brilliance.

This philosophy encourages you to celebrate others' success and progress rather than feeding into your own ego. It's about fostering a culture of teamwork and collaboration, where everyone can grow. But, of course, balance is key. No ego doesn't mean you're everyone's best friend or too soft; you still need to lead with strength and make tough calls when necessary.

We try our best to embody this mix of humility, excellence and humour. You work hard to build client relationships, deliver high quality projects, and nurture your team's growth, but you keep the mood light and maintain self-awareness. This aligns with the famous Buttface Meetings described by Phil Knight in his memoir, *Shoe Dog.* These meetings were anything but ordinary...Nike's leaders would gather around, toss their wildest ideas on the table, and then proceed to low key roast each other with brutal honesty. And yet, amidst the laughter, the jabs, and the occasional bruised ego, there was also some magic.

The beauty of *Buttface Meetings* wasn't just the humour and camaraderie...it was the underlying belief that nothing was too sacred to challenge, and no one was too important to laugh at themselves. They stripped away pretence and hierarchy, creating an environment where creativity flourished because people weren't afraid to be vulnerable. They were willing to laugh at themselves, take constructive criticism on the chin and value progress over perfection.

This approach proves that great work and humour don't just coexist...they fuel each other. The light-hearted atmosphere at Nike didn't dilute their drive for success, it fuelled it. By keeping things real, embracing humour, and focusing on work rather than egos, they created a culture where bold ideas thrive, and risks were rewarded.

I talk about what success looks like to me in a future chapter...but there's an example I want to touch on here that's relevant to what I'm talking about. Success is about the small, everyday moments that, at first glance, don't seem like much...but when you really stop and think about them, they're everything.

There's an ad I love that captures this perfectly. It's a McCain ad featuring comedian Becky Lucas, built around the idea of celebrating 'nothing special'...those unremarkable, everyday moments that actually mean the most. Pizza night with the kids. A bowl of chips on the couch with someone you love. These aren't the kind of things we put on a highlights reel, but when we look back, they're the moments that matter.

Karen Ramsay, McCain's head of communications, summed it up perfectly when she said, *"McCain is a brand that has never taken itself too seriously. We stand for great food that's comforting, brings people together, and is relaxed and messy—in a fun way!"* That really resonates with me, because at Paint It Black, we have a similar outlook. We take our work seriously, but we don't take *ourselves* too seriously. We believe in doing great work, looking after people, and making sure we have a laugh along the way.

That's what success feels like to me. Not some big, cinematic achievement...just real life, done well. A business that provides for my family, a workplace where people feel valued, and a bit of time to enjoy the ride along the way. It's not about being perfect or getting everything right; it's about showing up, giving a shit, and making sure the people around you know you do. Because in the end, it's not the awards or the bank balance you'll remember...it's the pizza nights.

For leaders and teams alike, the lesson is clear: don't take yourself so seriously that you stifle innovation. Sometimes, the best ideas come not from a stiff boardroom discussion, but from spirited debates where people aren't afraid to speak their minds, laugh at their mistakes, and stay focused on the bigger picture. And let's not forget...whether we're leading a global brand or managing a team of painters, it's important to keep perspective. We're painting houses, not curing cancer.

That simple reminder keeps us grounded. When humility and humour guide us, we can tackle even the toughest challenges without losing sight of the fact, at the end of the day, it's just paint... and there's always another wall to roll tomorrow.

King Regards

In the spirit of Nike's famous Buttface Meetings, where humour, honesty, and sharp wit were the foundations of their culture, we've found our own version of this ethos in the day-to-day chaos of running Paint It Black. Humour keeps us grounded, reminds us not to take ourselves too seriously, and lets us roll with the punches...whether it's a spray gun mishap or an email faux pas. And nothing exemplifies this better than the comedic duo of two of our supervisors, Billy and Ed, our very own bickering married couple who prove that great partnerships thrive on both respect and relentless banter.

When we set up our new office, it was spacious, with three private offices and two open areas. Naturally, these two decided to cram themselves into the same room. Why? Probably because they can't survive without bickering all day.

"It's freezing in here," Billy would complain, to which Ed would deadpan, "Clean your shoes, you pig". The daily updates were gold, with business sandwiched between hilarious jabs at each other. Billy would report: *"All Great Ocean Road jobs are going well. Might need to pinch someone from Geelong to finish the Lorne job tomorrow to meet this deadline. Oh, and did Ed tell you he has a girlfriend now? I found out through someone on this site today. Ed's being a little bitch and won't tell me anything. Also, can you ask him to change the radio station? I'm sick of sports talkback."*

Meanwhile, Ed's updates were equally peppered with ridicule: *"Sandringham job progressing well, just waiting on confirmation about the polished plaster and whether we need to undercoat it. Oh, and Billy returned his coffee today because it wasn't strong enough. Was very embarrassing."*

And then I'd have an update from Billy, *"That invoice for Dorman St is ready to send. Did you hear that Ed accidentally signed off with King Regards yesterday instead of Kind Regards?"* And on and on it went.

But the true essence of their partnership shone in moments like the infamous *"baby voice"* incident. One day, Ed called me, laughing so hard he could barely speak. I could barely understand him between wheezes. "Billy just did the cringiest thing ever," he began. In the background, I could hear Billy's yelling, "Shut up, Ed!" His voice sounded a mix, somewhere between frustration and mortification. Ed composes himself through his laughter, enough to continue with the story. "So, Billy just called the scissor lift company, right? And he hears this guy pick up the phone, but the guy doesn't exactly have the deepest voice. Billy thinks it's a kid. So, this is what I hear"...Ed pauses, trying not to laugh again. Then he launches into his perfect imitation of Billy. "'Hi, it's Billy from Paint It Black. Do you mind putting your mum or dad on, please?'"

Ed could barely contain himself, and I could almost picture Billy, red-faced and dying inside as the person on the other end of the phone stammered back, "Oh, I am the manager?" Billy had fumbled through an apology, before awkwardly proceeding to book the scissor lift.

"Mate, I've never seen someone's face drain of colour so quickly!" Ed cackled. "You should have heard the baby voice."

I could hear Billy in the background, voice rising, "Because he did! He sounded like a 10-year-old!"

I could only laugh and shake my head, grinning, knowing they'd spend the week ribbing each other over it.

And then came the email disaster.

It started with a seemingly simple request. A real estate agent reached out to both Billy and I, asking for quotes on some last-minute touch-ups. The job didn't sound great...low budget, tight deadlines, and rough suburbs. I was drafting up a polite decline when my inbox dinged.

There it was. The subject line hadn't even changed. Billy had replied all.

"THIS JOB DOESN'T EXIST. NEVER HEARD OF IT. I'M SICK OF GETTING THESE RANDOM REQUESTS FROM REAL ESTATE AGENTS FOR JOBS THAT DON'T EXIST!"

I stared at my screen, mouth open, unsure if I wanted to laugh or cry. Before I could even process it, my phone had lit up. Ed's name flashed on the screen.

"Did you just see what Billy wrote?" he said, the moment I answered.

Ed was roaring with laughter now, "He's sitting in the corner in the foetal position".

Meanwhile, my phone buzzed with a follow up email from Billy: *"Apologies, Anna, I misread your message. I thought it was from someone else. We would be delighted to quote your work. Please call me at your earliest convenience."*

The grovelling had begun.

Another ding. Another email. This time from Anna. *"It's fine. I can find someone else."*

And still, Billy couldn't leave it alone. Another email landed. *"I'm so sorry for the misunderstanding. Please reconsider. We'd love to work with you!"*

I couldn't even look at my laptop at this point. My phone buzzed again...this time, a text from Ed: *"Get this man a shovel"*.

Mistakes like this could deflate you. Make you want to throw your laptop and phone in front of a bus. The kind of memory that pops into your mind the moment you've forgotten about it. Billy's email bomb was a colossal misstep, but he owned it, and we all moved on. Ed's enjoyment? Well, that's just part of their dynamic, and honestly, it keeps us all entertained.

But beyond the humour, these stories reflect something deeper about who we aim to be as a company. My sister introduced a brilliant system to make sure we were living up to who we wanted to be...not some corporate version of ourselves, but the real us. We ditched the dry, robotic corporate speak that doesn't fit our personalities. Instead of signing off emails with *"Kind Regards"* (or, in Ben's case, accidentally typing "King Regards"), we switched to *"Cheers"*. Instead of saying, *"Our work is guaranteed to meet your expectations,"* we say, *"We're pumped to bring this to life"*. *"Excited to collaborate"* became *"Stoked to be involved"*. We even renamed our tender submissions to, "Don't Just Take Our Word For It".

We take our work seriously, but we don't take *ourselves* too seriously. Why would we? Pretending to be something we're not would only make us a poorer version of someone else. We're embracing the idea that authenticity beats perfection. Mistakes happen, laughter follows, and above all, we're still trying to deliver quality work while staying true to who we are. Because, as the saying goes, *"Be yourself; everyone else is taken"*. And, let's be honest, no one else could quite pull off what Billy and Ed bring to the table.

CHAPTER 7

DON'T BE AN OSTRICH

It's a bit ironic, isn't it? I just wrapped up the last chapter poking fun at corporate lingo and practices, and here I am, starting this one with a metaphor straight out of *Corporate Business 101*. But hey, sometimes those classic examples hit the mark. Small businesses can learn a lot from corporate philosophies, just as corporate teams could take a page or two from the humility and humour of small business life.

So, let's talk about the myth of the ostrich burying its head in the sand to avoid danger.

The myth suggests that ostriches bury their heads in the sand to avoid danger, thinking that if they can't see the threat, it doesn't exist.

The image of an ostrich with its head buried in the ground perfectly illustrates what happens when managers avoid dealing with poor performance. The ostrich may feel safe because it's blocked out the danger, but the threat hasn't gone anywhere. Likewise, a manager who sidesteps confronting issues might feel temporarily relief, but the problem is still there...festering, growing and eventually wreaking havoc.

Burying your head in the sand doesn't make the danger disappear. It just leaves you vulnerable. Ignoring poor performance is the same...it doesn't fix itself. In fact, it usually gets worse, leading to even bigger challenges (and problems) down the road.

The key takeaway here is simple: Confront issues head-on. Avoiding a tough conversation might feel easier in the moment, but it only prolongs the inevitable and makes the problem harder to fix.

It's natural to avoid confrontation. I hate being combative. I dread it...but the actual conversations aren't as bad as the mental buildups you've created in your head. The worry, the overthinking, the sleepless nights...it's all unnecessary. When you finally address the issue, you often find that the person on the other side was expecting it, or maybe if you're lucky, grateful for the clarity.

Facing problems early not only prevents them from spiralling...it shows you care enough to address the hard stuff. And honestly, once you get through that initial discomfort, you'll wonder why you didn't do it sooner.

At the end of the day, managing is a lot like painting. If you see a crack in the surface, you can't just ignore it and slap a fresh coat over the top. *Apologies for the shit painting metaphor.* It's always better to sand it back and fix the problem at the core. *Make it stop.*

You Must Do What Is Right, Not What Is Easy

This time, I was an ostrich. Dealing with this apprentice was a real challenge. He was smart, funny, and loved by everyone...including me. His quick wit and talent made him a standout. He could fix anything, a natural problem solver, and could even re-build spray guns. He picked up everything much easier than most.

Socially, he was the life of the party. The kind of guy who'd call into Triple J's Lunchtime Legend segment, request a song, and give shout-outs to the whole crew. He rocked up to our end of year boat party wearing a ridiculous captain's hat like he owned the place. At drag bingo, he was the first one up on stage, fully embracing the absurdity of the moment. He had this infectious energy that made him a magnet for fun. On the surface, he was a golden employee with massive potential.

But beneath the charm, he was becoming a problem. He started messing around with timesheets. He'd say he was running to the paint shop, when in reality, he'd head home or take a two-hour lunch break. The issue wasn't just his laziness; it was how his behaviour was spreading to others. Other apprentices started following his lead, cutting corners and clocking off early. What started as a personal issue turned into a team-wide problem.

I let things slide for too long, partly because of his likeability and partly because I didn't want to rock the boat. Whenever I'd talk to him about it, we'd end up laughing and the seriousness of the conversation got lost. It wasn't until his behaviour started creating tension among the team that I realised I had to act.

When I finally sat him down for a proper chat, he said all the right things and we got a sugar hit of a good citizen. Though he briefly straightened up, the damage had been done. His habits were now ingrained, and the trust was gone. Nobody wanted him on their job sites.. clients included. And eventually, I had no choice but to fire him. I often wonder how things would've been different if I'd handled it sooner...if I'd set firmer boundaries instead of letting things slide. You need to trust people's actions... not their words.

The firing itself was messy...a reflection of my lack of strength in handling these situations at the time. I was in Melbourne, and he was in Geelong, and I wasn't due back there for a week. Instead of making the trip to see him face-to-face, I called him. Maybe that wasn't the best idea. I just wanted it over...didn't want to sit on it any longer than I already had. I could hear the shift in his tone during the conversation...the respect dwindling as he processed that this big moment was being handled over the phone. Did I owe him the courtesy of doing it in person? *I don't know...maybe.*

But at the same time, he'd been lying to my face for weeks. "Yeah, I was working all morning," he'd say, even though I knew for a fact he wasn't. So maybe he wasn't worth the drive back to Geelong. It's a tough one. Over time, though, I've learned to handle these conversations much better.

The key is to be precise and professional. Most people don't want to be in this conversation either, so there's no need to ramble or sugarcoat it. These days, I stick to the facts: *"You received a warning on this date, and a second warning on this day. This is the reason for the decision."* That way, you're legally protected, and you're being clear. Then I outline the next steps...when they'll be paid out, what company property they need to return, and how this is the end of the line. This would have already been written up and ready to send to clarify.

But this firing wasn't like that. It was messy and soft, unfair on both of us. I rambled. "I don't want to do this, mate, but put yourself in my position." I even offered him two weeks of work to help him find a new job, promise I won't tell anyone I fired him. He tried to grovel, but at least I managed to find enough backbone to tell him the decision was final.

As I hung up the phone, I felt drained. The silence afterwards made me think of the words I scrambled to put together made no sense. My mind raced to thoughts of how it could have gone better. I pictured myself in Geelong, sitting across from him, calmly explaining the facts, offering closure rather than confusion.

The problem with burying your head in the sand is that eventually, you have to pull it out, and by then, the mess has usually grown bigger. In this case, it wasn't just about one apprentice...it was the ripple effect his actions had on the team. By avoiding the tough conversation, I let standards slip across the board, and it took time to wrestle them back.

Could I have knocked this on the head earlier? Maybe. Or maybe he was always going to self-destruct, and I was just delaying the inevitable. We'll never know. But what I *do* know is this: when burying your head in the sand, it doesn't take long for things to snowball...whether it's timesheets that don't add up, morale dropping amongst your team (*If he can get away with that, I might try),* or clients quietly questioning your professionalism.

Looking back on his time with us, it's clear...I was like an ostrich, burying my head in the sand, avoiding the difficult conversations because it was easier in the moment. Face the tough stuff early, even if it feels awkward or uncomfortable. It won't always guarantee a happy ending, but it gives you the best chance to protect your standards. Dumbledore's words ring true. *"You must do what is right, not what is easy."*

Eat the Frog

Let's stick with the animal metaphors for a moment. You've probably seen this one pop up in a corporate 'how-to' book or even in one of those endless LinkedIn post that I love so much.

The metaphor *eat the frog* is all about tackling your most difficult or unpleasant task first thing in the day. The idea is simple...if you had to eat a live frog, wouldn't it be better to just get it over and done with rather than letting it loom over you all day? It's often credited to Mark Twain, who said, *"If it's your job to eat a frog, it's best to do it first thing in the morning. And if it's your job to eat two frogs, it's best to eat the biggest one first."*

I think about this metaphor often, especially when there's something that could be done in under two minutes. Don't put it off, don't add it to a to-do list...just do it now. Make that call, respond to that email, eat the frog!

Now, I'll admit, there isn't a specific story tied to this one...I haven't been able to link back a drunk night at the footy, a prison shutdown, or painting the wrong house to a frog. In saying that, I'm sure we can all relate to this, probably most days...probably this moment. We're always procrastinating. I can think of five examples today without even trying.

There's the parking fine I've had stuffed in my pocket for five days. Every time I pull it out, it's like the ticket is judging me: *"Still here, mate?"* It'd take two minutes to pay and yet there it remains. Then there's an email about a painting quote I need to reply to. It's not even a hard one...literally organise a time to do it and it's done. Oh, and my mate I haven't called back, a birthday present for Dad, and a plant that I promised I'd help my wife, Edwina, re-pot weeks ago. Stupid frogs, just sitting there croaking at me.

The worst part is that doing these things would reduce any anxiety. The feeling of being in control, on top of things, albeit a moment, feels good. But still, I'll delay them to scroll through my phone.

In fact, I recently deleted all my social media apps to get better at this. And it worked...for about three hours. Then I caught myself scrolling through my photos, reading old notes, checking the weather. Turns out, you can take the apps away, but the procrastinator in you will find a way.

The truth is, I know I'm not following my own advice all the time, but here's the thing: the *'frog-eating'* strategy really does work. The days I actually do, knocking off the hardest or most annoying task first, the rest of the day feels easier, more manageable.

So why don't I do it all the time? Good question. Maybe it's because we're human, and frogs are gross. Maybe it's a conversation for someone who's a lot smarter than me on a much deeper level. Maybe, we're all masochists who love the chaos of a looming to-do list.

What I do know is this: the frogs don't eat themselves. And as much as we might joke about procrastination, there's a fine line between letting things sit for a minute and letting things spiral out of control. If I'd just paid the parking fine the day I got it, I wouldn't have spent five days feeling guilty every time I reached into my pocket.

So, here's to *eating the frogs*, one slimy task at a time. Maybe I'll start by re-potting that plant with Edwina. Or maybe, I'll check the weather first. Just in case.

CHAPTER 8

THE ART OF DELEGATING

It's so easy to fall into the trap of just doing everything yourself. You know exactly how you want it done, you know you can do it quicker, and let's face it, you probably think nobody can do it better. I've been there plenty of times...it feels natural, especially when you're busy, just to take it all on. But that approach might get you through the day; it won't get you through the years. It's unsustainable for both you and your team if you're serious about growth.

The challenge isn't just doing the work; it's about teaching someone else to do it just as well...or even better. Teaching takes time, patience, and energy, and in the moment, it can feel easier to skip it all together. But when you invest in showing someone else how to do it properly, you're making a long-term play. Sure, they might make mistakes along the way, and yes, those mistakes can be frustrating and slow you down. But every time you teach, you're not just building the r skills...you're building a team that can absorb some of the load.

Delegation isn't about dumping work on someone else's desk; it's about giving them the tools and trust to handle it. It's a process, and it's not always smooth, but the alternative is worse: you end up burnt out, and the team stays dependent on you for every little thing. And here's the kicker...if mistakes are made, that's on you. If they didn't get it right, ask yourself: did I take the time to explain it properly? Did I show them what 'good' looks like? If the answer is no, then the problem isn't just them...it's your leadership.

I've also learned that if you can't explain your work or your vision clearly, you'll struggle to bring anyone else along with you. Leadership isn't just about knowing what needs to be done, it's about communicating in a way that makes others want to get on board. If you've got a well thought out plan, but no execution, you're just dreaming. If you can execute but don't inspire or stand for anything bigger than yourself, you've missed the point of leadership entirely.

The truth is... teaching sharpens your own skills too. When you explain something to someone else, you're forced to think about it more deeply and identify areas you might have overlooked. It creates a culture of shared knowledge, and when you've got a team that's learning, growing, and stepping up, the whole operations become stronger, more agile, and more capable.

It's also important to have diversity and different viewpoints in decision making. Pat Cummins (*another Pat reference*) nails a fundamental truth in his book, *Tested*, when he talks about treating everyone like adults. Their team motto, *'Control your own space,'* isn't about hands-off leadership; it's about trust and autonomy, and respecting the individuality of each person on the team. Essentially, it says, *"We're not going to babysit you. You know what's best for you...personally and professionally...so step up and own it."* That philosophy not only empowers people but also builds a deeper sense of accountability.

It ties back to trust, something we've spoken about in earlier chapters. But it's more than that...it's about the autonomy you give your team and the leadership you draw out of them. When you trust your people to manage themselves, you're giving them permission to step into their own potential, and you're signalling that you believe in their ability to make decisions. You're also creating space for diversity of thought, which is critical.

Teams are made up of different personalities, and we should look at that positively. That's the beauty. Diversity isn't just a corporate buzzword, it's critical for growth. As Pat highlights, the best teams are made up of people who wear different hats...whether it's the reliable ones who get things done no matter what, the curious ones who are always questioning and innovating, or the funny circuit breakers who lighten the mood when tensions are high.

You need the curious ones who will throw out fifty wild ideas, knowing forty-nine might miss the mark, but that one could be pure gold. You need experienced hands who've been through battles before and can provide calm guidance. And yes, you need reliable ones, the steady operators who make sure the wheels don't fall off. But you also need that joker, the one who can diffuse a tense room and bring a bit of perspective when things feel overwhelming.

The strength of the team lies in the diversity...not just in backgrounds or demographics but in ways of thinking, problem-solving, and communicating. If everyone on your team was the same, you'd flatline. A team of reliable, conservative thinkers might never take the risk needed to unlock potential growth. A team of bold-risk takers might burn the whole thing down.

At the end of the day, growth doesn't come from you doing everything...it comes from stepping back, teaching, and trusting others to take the reins. It's a humbling process, and sometimes it's messy, but it's the only way forward if you want to build something bigger than yourself.

A Crash Course in Humility

I normally don't mind flying, but this trip was different. From the very moment we arrived behind schedule at Terminal 2 Melbourne Airport, to the very instant where I was confined to my seat, with my seatbelt on as the aircraft stampeded through an impenetrable sky. I'd loathed the whole process this day... standing in line, checking your bags in, standing in line, customs, standing in line, passport control, standing in line. I loathed the engine started up as the colossal beast trundled around the tarmac, the overkill of energy pushing you back in your seat as it springs onward and escapes the earth and mounts the universe. The ground moves further and further away while you pierce through a layer of clouds. Seven hundred tons soaring above the Earth from one side of the world to the other like a bird. I was loathing the crying babies and the paella that tasted like a leather boot. The passenger next to me had his aircon on the highest level carrying the refrigerated air straight onto me. The egocentric passenger in front of me thought it was fine to have his seat all the way back the moment the plane was in the air and the kid behind me thought he was in a karate fight and wouldn't stop booting the back of my chair. I started playing Who Wants to Be a Millionaire but slipped up on the thousand-dollar question. I caught my passenger sitting under his full blasted arctic air throw a look at me, that said, "You should have locked in C you dickhead, you have two floating ribs". Fair to say, I was a bit anxious about leaving the business for three weeks for a holiday in Europe.

The decision to take a holiday felt like a coup against my own sanity. At Berlin Airport, I stood there, waiting for my bags, but with the distinct feeling I'd forgotten to pack one crucial item...a double dose of blind faith in my team back home. It hit me like a bourbon hangover...had I really prepared my second in command to fill my shoes? Or was I about to hand them a grenade and hope they knew which end was the pin?

THE ART OF DELEGATING

Up until that moment, I thought I had it figured out. I had a good grasp on what success looked like to me. Keep the number healthy enough, make a decent wage, and pull off a few trips each year without feeling like I had separation anxiety from the business. It was a straightforward formula...success to me was freedom. Being able to get away, play some golf on a Wednesday when the sun was out. Flexibility and freedom...that was success. But as I sat in the cab on the way into Berlin, Paint It Black was now a system that relied too heavily on me.

For most of my career up until this point, the team could be counted on one hand, and going away was no Herculean task. Run the payroll ahead of time, tell clients I'd be unreachable, put my out of office email on with the phone number of one of the workers to contact and put that same someone in charge of the schedule... and hope for the best. In that setup, things could only go sideways. But this time, flying over the Indian Ocean, and for reasons I couldn't yet articulate, I felt I was abandoning a very intricate web that I'd become the sole spider of, despite myself.

In hindsight, the whole experience was humbling. When I returned, everything was still standing. My team managed, jobs got done, clients didn't revolt. It was a crash course in humility...maybe I wasn't as important as I thought I was!

The year before my next holiday, I made a vow: the next time I went away, I was not going to suffer separation anxiety from my business. It wasn't just about enjoying an enchilada with my wife and friends in Mexico without refreshing emails or worrying about what might be going wrong. I knew that by letting go and truly stepping away, I could unknowingly unlock another level of growth for the business. New ideas could flow in, people would step up in ways they hadn't before, and problems would be absorbed and solved without me as a safety net. It wasn't just about taking a holiday...it was about making the business stronger, more resilient, and less reliant on me.

That became my mission. I had twelve months to make it happen, and I treated it like my number one priority. I realised that my anxiety levels on holiday would directly correlate to how well I'd prepared the team in the months leading up. If I wanted a relaxing trip, I had to put in the work beforehand.

The first step was investing in my second-in-command. I went through everything I had to make sure he was ready to take the reins. It wasn't just about giving him responsibility; it was about giving them the tools, the guidance, and the confidence to run the show without me. I didn't want to be replying to emails while choking on tacos in a state of panic...I wanted to pack my bags knowing that my business was in good hands.

Turns out, he was more than ready...and if I'm being honest, I was probably the one holding him back. The same when I started investing more in other leaders in the business. Maybe people get to these positions for a reason? When I finally gave them the space to lead, they didn't just fill the gap...I realised they were better equipped than I'd given them credit for.

That meant delegating more than ever before, even when it would have been quicker or easier to do things myself. It meant sitting down with leaders to work through scenarios, passing on knowledge I'd gathered over the years, being patient when mistakes happened. I had to remind myself that every mistake was a learning opportunity...both for them and me.

I was at a business conference recently...you know the type. Big, air-conditioned room with those hotel carpets that are trying way too hard to be interesting. I ordered a latte and flat white for someone I was there with, and two of the exact same coffees got made. The room had the smell of burnt coffee, freshly printed nametags, and the slightly nervous energy of people trying to network.

THE ART OF DELEGATING

The speaker for the session steps up...one of Gillian McLachlan's former team members. The chatter of the room dies down as people shuffle into their seats that are slightly too close together. "Working with Gill was..." she pauses for dramatic effect, "an experience". She chuckles at herself.

She goes on to describe Gill as a powerhouse of a leader...sharp, measured, and so in control that it seemed like he could solve a crisis before anyone even knew there was one. "The smartest guy in the room, every single time. He also gets people. Can lead or talk to anyone. The classy performer you all see on TV and radio, is what we get behind closed doors too," she says, seemingly lost in admiration.

But then she adds, "The thing about Gill though...he can't let go. It's his fatal flaw." I lean in to listen more intently...Gil doesn't look like someone with a flaw.

The speaker launches into a story. She paints the scene: a massive scandal has broken out in the AFL, the kind that makes headlines and sends every footy fan into a frenzy. "So, we jump on this emergency zoom call," she says, "And here's Gill. He's sitting there in a short sleeved floral party shirt, sunglasses perched on his head, the ocean literally sparkling behind him. And I'm immediately caught off guard because he's forever sporting a suit. Someone goes, 'Gil, where the hell are you?' And he just casually says, 'Oh, yeah I'm in Hawaii.' Like it's no big deal."

The speaker shakes her head, grinning, "He was on holiday and didn't tell anyone. And this wasn't the first time he'd just go on holiday, and it would be easier for him to just not tell anyone and continue to do his job...heaven forbid anyone could step up." The last bit comes out a bit sassy.

The absurdity of it all made me laugh, and it also struck a chord. As the speaker wrapped up, "Look, Gill was brilliant. The best I've ever worked with. But even he had to work on trust and letting go. Because if you don't, eventually you'll end up juggling a crisis from a beach chair in Hawaii."

The room clapped and I couldn't help but reflect. There's something comforting about knowing that even Gill McLachlan...arguably one of the most capable leaders in the country...had his struggles stepping back. He had no shortage of quality that he could draw upon but still thought that it was just easier to do shit himself.

It wasn't easy to step back. Letting go of control isn't exactly in my nature. But over time, I saw the benefits. People stepped up in ways I didn't expect. Solutions I would never have thought of emerged because different perspectives were being brough to the table. And while I was still there to guide and mentor, I wasn't the only one putting out the fires.

When the time came for that next trip...three glorious weeks in Mexico...I felt like I earned the right to relax. I could swim in a cenote, sip a margarita, and know that the wheels wouldn't fall off while I was gone. Even better, stepping back allowed me to see the bigger picture. I came back with new ideas, fresh energy, and a renewed sense of purpose.

Now with thirty people at the time of writing, it's no longer a choice but a necessity to scale and empower others. As much as I love being hands-on, growth has forced my role to shift. A happy by-product of this scaling up is the structure and operational setups that we've put in place to keep things running smoothly. Processes are no longer dependent on me being there every day because we've built solid systems, trusted routines, and a team that understands how things should work without needing constant oversight.

The transition has been humbling, but it's a game-changer in terms of freedom and flexibility. The team's capable of keeping momentum, making critical decisions, and, most importantly, operating independently of me in the day-to-day. It turns out that creating a business that isn't entirely dependent on its founder has not only strengthened our operation but also allowed me to step away and trust that things won't go to shit because I'm not on site.

I still struggle with the handover. It's tough to step back from something you've built from the ground up, knowing that it's being steered by someone else, however capable. But I've learned what works to keep me less anxious while I'm away. All I need is a daily update, just a quick report from all the supervisors and a summary of our second in command, a note to let me know everything is cruising. And if it's not, this is what we're doing about it. That's all I need...to not be in the dark. Now, success for me is minimising headaches as much as possible. Strict policies on who we work with, a hard pass on high-maintenance clients, and a healthy respect for red flags. Because really, what's the point of all this hard work if you can't check out every now and again?

CHAPTER 9

KEEP DOING, STOP DOING, START DOING

Leadership is often seen as guiding others, setting the vision, and driving the team forward. But how often do we, as leaders, pause to examine ourselves with the same level of scrutiny we apply to our teams? Leadership isn't a one-way street. At a glance, leadership can look like it has all the answers. It should feel more like asking the right questions...of others, yes, but also of ourselves. How am I showing up? What am I missing? Am I even living the values? These are tough questions to ask, and even tough to answer honestly.

An external review is one of the most powerful ways to start this process, which I'll get to in the next story...but they can be done internally and continuously too. It's like holding up a mirror...not the flattering Instagram-filter kind either, maybe one of those snapchat filters that turns you into a bit of a goose. But it's a good way to find out what's working and what's not. Find any blind spots. If we expect our team to embrace growth, welcome feedback, and continuously improve, we as leaders need to be open to the same level of scrutiny and self-development.

In many workplaces, feedback flows one way: from leadership to the team. Leaders, however, often sidestep this level of structured critique. We put an emphasis on accountability and communication. And in the review process we use a scoring system to evaluate each job out of 100 based on criteria that reflect our core values in a job: quality, no call-backs, project coordination, cleanliness, safety, profitability, deadlines, communication, client satisfaction, supervisory skills and team oversight...there's also points up for grabs for marginal gains like positivity, how well they interact with our project app and pride they've taken in the job. The scoring system has proven to be an effective tool for awarding bonuses to those that excel and align with our standards. It's also a great training tool, giving us clear, actionable insights into where our supervisors need to improve. This process holds everyone accountable, motivates continuous growth, and allows us to recognise high performance and address any gaps in a structured way. But it can't all be one way... as leaders, we need to be held to the same account.

By undergoing a review of ourselves, we're not just inviting feedback but are actively seeking insights that may reveal blind spots...issues that may be impacting our leadership or our team's performance without us realising it. This isn't just about external advice; it's about gaining a fresh perspective on aspects we may be too close to see.

We know the business intimately, but we're also susceptible to our own biases and limitations. An outside perspective can highlight areas we might be overlooking or handling less effectively than we'd like to admit. By confronting these hidden issues and addressing them directly, we strengthen our leadership and build a culture of openness, accountability, and growth across the company. It's an opportunity to lead by example.

KEEP DOING, STOP DOING, START DOING

We've tried just about every way under the sun to review ourselves and get feedback from the team. We've done surveys...long and detailed ones, quick pulse checks, named and anonymous versions. We've held town hall style meetings, one-on-ones, and sometimes even cracked open a few beers and let Dutch courage do its thing (more on that in the next story). Every approach has its merits and challenges. In ask me anything sessions, the louder personalities tend to dominate. Anonymous feedback can be harder to follow up or dig into for the root cause. Surveys with names attached sometimes result in overpolite, sugar-coated responses, and one on ones can be tricky if someone is shy or reluctant to open up. Still, you have got to keep at it. And more importantly act on it. I feel when we invite feedback, and someone has the courage to speak up, not acting on it – or at least addressing it with an explanation – puts you in an even worse position.

The most productive style is one we use amongst our leadership team... it is a simple but impactful feedback exercise: identifying what I'd like each person to keep doing (positive reinforcement), what to start doing (introducing a new skill or improving on something underdeveloped), and what to stop doing (correcting or eliminating behaviours). This format has proven to be a powerful, straightforward way to foster development. I've found that not only does it encourage positive behaviour, but it also opens a two-way conversation that can reveal a person's reasoning behind their actions, often illuminating motivations or constraints I may not have been aware of.

For instance, I recently challenged one of our leaders on his reluctance towards new tasks. He explained that his pushback was rooted in his belief that someone was more suited for the task, and his skillset was better applied elsewhere. He mentioned that he did enjoy the challenge of getting out of the office...just that he thought his strengths were better leveraged in his current role. While I disagreed on some of his points, it was valuable to understand his honest perspective. This kind of candid feedback is insightful; it builds trust and keeps us aligned on our goals.

Of course, feedback needs filtering. In the spirit of The Man in the Arena chapter, I try to value insights from people whose opinions I trust, instead of unsolicited advice...like at a Christmas party when a few drinks loosen tongues. Constructive feedback, though, is invaluable; I've been told, for instance, that I can act too quickly without consulting others. It's not that I'm careless or dismissive...I feel like I'm just wired to move fast. When I decide something needs doing, I must do it that instant...and I'm often halfway through the process before I've completely weighed up all the options. One time, for example, I decided on a whim to re-turf the backyard. Within minutes, I had hired a rotary hoe, driven to Reece Plumbing to buy irrigation supplies, started a group chat called 'lawn porn', and was back home tearing up the lawn. That night, under floodlights, I found myself knee-deep in a backyard that was a long way from ready for turf the next day. What was supposed to be a quick, efficient job turned into a drawn-out process full of frustration, and now, ribbing from my mates in the group chat that I used the wrong grass. *Don't use Buffalo, thick as shit. Why couldn't you use Kikuya?* All because I skipped over a few key steps in my eagerness to get it done.

It's a classic *'red trait'*, as described in the book, *Surrounded by Idiots*. People with strong 'red' personalities are decisive, action-orientated, and driven to achieve results...great for getting things done quickly. But the flipside of this strength is a tendency to bulldoze through tasks without enough planning or consultation. *Red* thrives on momentum, which can sometimes come at the cost of patience or foresight.

For me, it often feels natural to jump straight into action. The feedback reminded me that I need to pause and gather input from others. I've had to learn (and am still learning) that slowing down and seeking advice isn't a sign of weakness...it's a way to avoid unnecessary mistakes and bring others along for the ride.

The book *Surrounded by Idiots* didn't just help me understand my own tendencies; it opened my eyes to how others operate, and why they behave the way they do. Take *'blues'*, for example...the meticulous ones who want to read every word of a terms and conditions. *Blues* are reliable to the core. When they take on a task, you know it'll be done right, down to the last detail. But if you had a team full of blues, progress could crawl to a halt under the weight of perfectionism.

Then there are *'yellows'*...the life of the party types. Think of a natural born salesman, charismatic and able to sell sunscreen in Scotland. They light up a room and bring energy and creativity, but can also dominate conversation, overshadow others, and sometimes fail to follow through. They're full of big ideas but can be, as the saying goes, all duck and no dinner.

And *'greens'*... the most common personality type. The peacemakers. They avoid confrontation, prefer harmony, and will quietly carry the load to keep things running smoothly. *Greens* are dependable workhorses, but if you carry too many of them, you risk stagnation because no one wants to step up and lead or rock the boat.

What reading that book taught me is that the diversity of these personalities, when balanced, is what makes a team truly great. Reds drive action, blues ensure accuracy, yellows spark innovation, and greens provide stability. Too many of the same 'colour', though, and the balance is lost.

The reminder I got from my team's feedback is that empowering my leadership team means I need to pause and consult them more frequently. The 'keep, start, stop' method not only helps me get valuable insights from those I trust, but it also helps us grow together by building a culture of transparency, shared decision-making, and continuous improvement.

Feedback is essential. It's how we improve, grow, and get better at what we do. But there's a catch...not all feedback is created equal. If you invite the wrong people to the table, or if the setting isn't right, feedback can go from constructive to destructive in no time.

Take this story from Richmond Football Club as a perfect example. Back when the 'Leading Teams' strategy was first introduced, the idea was to create a culture of honesty...where players could sit in front of their teammates and receive feedback designed to help them improve. In theory, it made sense. In practice, at least early on, it could be brutal.

A 19-year-old player, fresh into the system and still learning his craft, found himself in the hot seat. What was supposed to be a structured, constructive session quickly turned into a pile-on. Instead of meaningful feedback about his game or work ethic, he was hit with personal attacks. "I don't mind you as a footballer, but as a bloke, I think you're a fuckwit." "You walk around the gym like you own the place...how about you shut up and do some fucking weights?" Even his fashion choices copped it: "You dress like a fucking flog".

There was nothing constructive about it...just a group of players who felt like they had to prove how brutally 'honest' they could be. The young player was completely isolated, left to wear the brunt of it on his own. A couple of teammates called him afterward to admit it had gone too far, but in the moment, no one stood up to stop it. Two years later, he was delisted, and he's since spoken about how long it took to rebuild his confidence.

Years later, Richmond would go on to become renowned for their strong team culture, and their feedback sessions became a real strength. But the difference? They learned how to do it properly. Emma Murray, their mindfulness coach, helped them shape an environment where feedback was still brutally honest at times, but constructive and respectful. Players left those meetings with a clearer sense of what they needed to improve, not just a shattered self-esteem.

The lesson here? Feedback is powerful, but only when it's given by the right people, in the right way, for the right reasons. If you invite feedback from people who aren't equipped to give it...or if the environment isn't set up for real growth...it can do more harm than good. So, be careful who you listen to. There's a big difference between feedback that helps you and feedback that just tears you down.

Don't Let Someone Borrow Your Watch to Tell You the Time

South of the Yarra...ah yes, the Promised Land for those with Range Rovers and cashmere sweaters draped over their shoulders. A separate state where everyone is vaccinated against the filth of the north. No old-school pubs with sticky carpets, no grungy craft breweries with mismatched furniture...just wine bars, boutique stores, and brunch spots where avocado reigns supreme.

I'd booked us into the College Lawn Hotel for the annual Paint It Black Christmas bash. If nothing else, I figured I'd be the boss who'd booked the cool place, right? Beer garden, cheeseburger sliders, seltzers on tap...everything the young folk love.

The day started off shaky, yet alarmingly high-octane. Our wildest worker had organised a champagne breakfast for those who thought twelve hours of drinking might be a bit tame. So, by the time I arrived, some of them didn't know if they were Arthur or Martha, eyes glazed, and grins stretched like Cheshire cats as the hot December sun bore down on the beer garden. The tension of a year's worth of grinding began melting away, replaced by a much stronger presence of tequila shots and espresso martinis. Our staff staggered and swayed in tune with the drunk crowd. The frenzy of it all!

I was leaning against the bar, half-heartedly nursing a beer, when I felt it coming...a small shift in energy, the subtle exchanges of banter threatening to evolve into something more pointed. It started small, like the first few drops of rain before a storm. One voice broke through the noise, casual but carrying just enough venom to hint at what was coming.

"Hey," someone slurred, leaning in closer than necessary, their breath a cocktail of rum and confidence. "Why isn't my bonus bigger? My old company gave me way more of an end of year bonus."

I sighed, thinking of a diplomatic way of saying, "Fuck off back to your old company then". Before I could even start, another voice jumped in, louder and more dramatic, "And what's with all these jobs in Melbourne you had me working at this year? It does my head in travelling an hour each way every day."

I glanced up, again thinking of a better way of saying, "I'll tell the clients to move their projects next door to your place".

The third wave hit before I could brace for it. Someone else, spilling a whisky, that I was paying for, sighed heavily and said, "I don't want to tell you what to do..." And of course, proceeded to tell me what the heck to do.

At some point over the next hour, the DJ began to play loud enough to drown them out. I was half listening, half wishing I was north of the river, closer to home. By the time the sun was beginning to set, the party was shot...if I had to hear one more thing about how to run Paint It Black, I was going to snap.

The next morning, I woke up with a head like a crushed can and a rapidly growing list of people I wanted to call. "Couldn't remember" was what they most said. I stewed over it all holiday, gnashing my teeth and vowing that next year we will do a day show and ban the champagne breakfast. No more free-for-all's south of the river where alcohol turned grievances into golden tickets for anyone with a complaint.

KEEP DOING, STOP DOING, START DOING

The new year brought a clean slate, so I reached out to Rach, a good friend and business powerhouse, who happened to be on maternity leave but was thankfully willing to take on a review of my business. She could've run my business in her sleep at that stage, but here she was, listening to me, sleepy-eyed and nodding, as I rattled on about external reviews and how they'd help root out all the bad apples. I thought she'd find the culprits; help identify the drama starters...maybe next year's Christmas party won't be so bad after all!

She listened and then just laughed. "Let me get this straight," she said, "You want me to tell you who's worth keeping and who's rocking the boat? You already know. Do you really want me to borrow your watch and tell you the time? What do you actually need?" She stopped me dead in my tracks. All I could manage was, "I feel like things could be done a bit easier". I wanted a business that ran itself while I took a holiday.

What Rach helped me figure out was when I started out, I was a painter. That's what I knew, and that's what I was good at. And this isn't unique to me ..ask most tradespeople or specialists who start a business, and you'll hear the same story. Whether it's painting, IT, landscaping, plumbing, or graphic design, the early days of your business are about doing the work you're skilled at. You've built a reputation on your craft, and that's what pays the bills. Sure, you might hire an accountant for tax time or get someone to help with payroll or basic admin, but for the most part, you're still out there in the thick of it, doing what you do best.

But then, almost without realising it, things start to change. You're good at what you do, and because of that, the work comes pouring in. Suddenly, you're not just the painter or landscaper or IT consultant...you're also a recruiter, hiring staff to help carry the load. Now you're learning about employment contracts, payroll systems, leave entitlements, and HR policies. You're trying to keep everyone busy, so you dip your toe into marketing, learning about advertising, social media, and branding. You're quoting more, managing more, and realising you need better systems to keep track of it all: timesheets, quality control, client feedback, job revisions, and analytics.

And then the shift happens. It's subtle at first. You're no longer spending most of your time on the thing you love...your craft. Instead, you're learning about LinkedIn, submitting tender documents, and creating safety management plans. Companies want to know about your environmental policies and community contributions. Suddenly, you're exporting spreadsheets and sitting in meetings about processes you didn't even know existed a few years ago. Then one day, you realise you've transitioned from being a painter, or whatever your trade is, to being a business operator, and it feels foreign.

For me, this was a massive adjustment. At one point, I looked around and realised I was only painting 10% of the time...the very thing that had gotten me here. The other 90% was spent on tasks that, quite honestly, I had no formal training for and often felt overwhelmed by. It's a challenge so many tradespeople and specialists face: figuring out how to navigate this shift and redefine where your time and energy need to go.

The truth is this transition doesn't happen overnight. You don't wake up one day and suddenly become an expert in business operations, marketing, HR, or IT. It's a process, and it's one that requires both self-awareness and a willingness to adapt. Some tasks, you'll find, come naturally or might even spark a new passion. For me, analysis and problem-solving fell into that category...I loved figuring out what was working, what wasn't, and how to improve. But even with the things I enjoyed, I didn't do it alone. I leaned on experts like Rach, who helped me upskill and provided guidance when I needed it.

Other tasks, like IT, weren't my forte and didn't ignite the same enthusiasm. In those cases, I reached out for help and kept those experts on the books, either as employees or subcontractors, to manage what I couldn't. The key was understanding where my strengths were, where I needed to upskill, and where it made more sense to delegate.

It all started with a shift in mindset: accepting that my role had evolved and that the skills I needed to succeed now weren't the same as when I'd first started.

I think that's important in an external review. Identify your blind spots and understand what you want to get out of it (*has one external review and thinks he's an expert*). You've got time to figure it out, and no one expects you to master everything from day one. The most important thing is to recognise when you need help, whether it's temporary guidance or ongoing support, and to embrace the idea what your role will keep evolving.

Looking back at that Christmas party, I can see it for what it was: a messy collision of frustration, beer-fuelled confidence, and a genuine (if poorly timed) desire to be heard. Nearly all of those feedback givers are now gone, and in hindsight, it was telling. Some of them were the very people who feature in the stories I'll share in the upcoming chapters about firing and making tough calls. They weren't the ones helping carry the business forward, and their behaviour that day was a red flag I hadn't fully recognised at the time.

But not all of it was bad. Some of the others who spoke up came to me afterward, sober and reflective, and apologised for the outburst. They admitted the timing was wrong but made it clear they genuinely wanted to be heard. That taught me something important: even when the delivery is all wrong, feedback often comes from a place of wanting to feel valued and understood. That messy afternoon opened lines of communication with those who truly cared about the business, and I was able to take something positive from it.

I'll admit, for a moment, I almost put a hard ban on champagne breakfasts. But in the end, I realised that wasn't the solution. You must treat people like adults and trust that over time, culture will naturally evolve with the right team in place. And it did. As the years passed and a few of those troublemakers left the business, the champagne breakfast drama left with them. Nowadays, I love a Christmas party. It's an unspoken rule now...keep it north of the river and don't talk shop all day...and it works because the team we've built is strong.

CHAPTER 10

HOW TO FAIL

Pat Cummins' style of leadership combines substance with values that are redefining Australian cricket. Not only could he play James Bond, but he also combines a great respect for the game with a quiet, confident strength...he doesn't need to sledge opponents or rely on the intimidation that once was synonymous with Australian cricket. His leadership goes beyond the field, too; he understands the pressure his teammates face and doesn't force them into the one shoe fits all, work hard, party harder mould that once dominated Aussie cricket culture.

He's also shown he won't be a traditionalist for tradition's sake. Pat challenges the norms: when he opted to bowl first in a World Cup final, ex-players blowing up on twitter across the country, *Australians bat first, always*!

Most impressively, when his players face criticism from former players or the media, he doesn't hesitate to stand by them, showing loyalty and integrity while still respecting different opinions. His loyalty to his players, paired with his personal ethics, make him a leader who commands respect by his actions. Take this example of leadership:

The tension surrounding Justin Langer's resignation as Australian cricket coach was a storm unlike anything Pat had faced as a leader at that point in time. The media frenzy, the verbal attacks from former players, and even Langer's own pointed remarks created a relentless pile-on, painting Pat and his team as soft and rebellious. But in amongst the chaos, Pat showed leadership that will forever stick with me.

From the outset, Pat refused to inflame the situation. He didn't make public comments while decisions were still being deliberated, respecting the process and keeping the sanctity of the dressing room intact. That alone was a mark of class. But when the time came to speak, he delivered a response that balanced respect, honesty, and unwavering loyalty to his team.

Cummins acknowledged Langer's intensity...a trait that came from a place of deep passion and love for the baggy green. He didn't shy away from praising Langer's contributions, calling him a legend of the sport whose drive had elevated team culture and standards. *"His intensity wasn't the issue,"* Cummins clarified. The players respected it. But the team had evolved, and the coaching style needed to evolve with it.

What made Cummins' response so remarkable wasn't just his clarity in articulating the team's position but the respect he extended to everyone involved, even to those attacking him. He thanked former players who had criticised him for their opinions, recognising their passion for the game and their loyalty to Langer as a teammate. But he also stood firm.

"Just as you've always stuck up for your mates," he said, *"I'm sticking up for mine."*

It was a powerful moment. In one sentence, Cummins encapsulated what leadership is all about: taking the hits, standing by your people, and doing what's right...even when it's not popular. He wasn't just defending his teammates; he was defining what his captaincy stood for.

Looking back, that line is what truly sets Pat apart. It wasn't an act of defiance or arrogance...it was a statement of values. He wasn't asking for validation or trying to win anyone over. That's why, despite the noise, Pat Cummins' leadership shone through. It wasn't about being the loudest voice in the room; it was about being the one who quietly made the hardest decisions while holding his head high. And in that moment, he proved that leadership isn't about pleasing everyone...it's about doing what's right for the people you lead...and staying true to what you believe in.

Pat isn't afraid to step into the role as clutch performer on the field either. He takes wickets when his team needs a breakthrough and adds runs when they're desperately needed, demonstrating that leadership is more than strategy...it's about showing up when it matters most. His reliability comes from his authenticity; he's tough yet approachable, principled yet willing to listen. He might not be perfect, but that only makes him relatable, proving that leadership isn't about being flawless.

Anyone on my team who hears me mention Pat Cummins again is probably rolling their eyes already...here we go again, guy is obsessed. And maybe they're right. I've even slapped his name on our training seminars and had to defend my Pat Cummins Leadership Seminars slides once or twice. His approach isn't just another lesson in how to lead; it's a blueprint for how to fail with dignity and purpose.

On a recent podcast, he laid out his philosophy beautifully. The current Australian cricket team is founded on aggressive, proactive mindset where taking calculated risks is prioritised over playing it safe. Pat has made it clear that his philosophy isn't just about winning but also about how the team approaches each game and each ball. He emphasises that if the team is going to fail, they should do so by playing boldly...not by holding back to avoid mistakes.

This ethos translates directly into Pat's bowling style, where he would rather attack the batter and risk conceding extra runs than bowl defensively just to protect his stats. Bowling with this level of aggression, even if it means occasionally leaking a few extra runs, reflects his belief that defence and conservatism rarely lead to impactful outcomes in the game.

The same with his batting. If he gets out being tentative...he has failed. If he gets out trying to be proactive and take the game on... that's fine, he can live with that.

The common theme when talking to or reading about a successful leader of sport or business...they'll always talk about failure as much as they do success.

Elizabeth Day, the celebrated British writer and host of How to Fail, has a refreshingly insightful take on the topic of failure. For many, failure feels like a label...a heavy, permanent tag that defines who they are. But Day argues that this mindset is fundamentally flawed. *"A lot of people wrongly believe failure defines them when it happens,"* she says. *"But actually, failure more often than not is something that happens to you."*

Her perspective is liberating. Day emphasises the importance of distancing ourselves from failure, recognising it not as an inherent characteristic but as an external event. *"We think we are failures,"* she explains, *"but usually failure is just something that happens to us. It's like anxiety...I am not my anxiety; it is just something that happens to me."* This shift in thinking reframes failure, stripping it of its power to consume us. Failures, no matter how big or small, must be acknowledged for what they truly are: events...nothing more, nothing less. They are not markers of who we are, but merely moments in time.

Day's analogy to anxiety is particularly striking because it underscores how our struggles often feel all-encompassing, even though they are just passing moments. Like a cloud that temporarily obscures the sun, failure might feel overwhelming, but it doesn't diminish the brightness that exists behind it. She reminds us that failure is not a personal flaw or a permanent state...it is simply part of the human experience. It's a reminder that while we may not have control over what happens to us, we do have control over how we respond. And in that response lies the opportunity to grow, learn, and ultimately, succeed.

And I think there's a lot we can take from that mindset. It's a powerful philosophy, especially when it comes to navigating the risk of business and leadership. You might think you've heard it all before, but taking these principles and applying them to how we lead, take risks, and handle setbacks...that's where the real gold is.

A Three-Day-Old Beer

Failure is a funny beast...always lurking, waiting for you to trip on your own ambition. I've danced with it enough times to know that failures teach you something. You don't lose, you learn.

Take this one time as a footy coach...The change rooms before a footy game are their own kind of chaotic symphony. The air is thick with the unmistakable scent of Deep Heat...sharp, medicinal, and oddly comforting. On the table in the middle of the room, there's a spread of lollies and fruit, and as always, I've already eaten way too many snakes before we've even warmed up. "Best two hours of the week, let's shop early!" Robbo yells from across the room. No one knows what it means, but we laugh every time. Another voice chimes in: "Don't lose at home". Right, because the extra 20 locals standing on the boundary are supposed to be some game-changing advantage.

The preparations are as diverse as the players themselves. Some are locked in, headphones on, eyes shut, in a personal pre-game ritual. Others are more casual, sharing a laugh, puffing on a smoke or sneaking in a vape outside the doors. Then there's our captain... good bloke, great leader...but prone to moments that leave you shaking your head. Today, he's just finished taping his left shoulder only to realise his right one is the injured one. Classic.

The gear sprawled across the room tells its own story. There's always a mix of backpacks, the occasional proper club-branded sports bag, and a few who've brought their boots and kit stuffed into mismatched shopping bags. You can't help but wonder about the lives behind those bags...22 blokes from all walks of life, with jobs, families, and God knows what else going on. For the next couple of hours, though, it's all about footy. This is their time to let it all out.

Our vice-captain, always the picture of intensity, looks like he's ready to devour the opposition. He also looks hungover? Meanwhile, three of our players...still in their work boots...are juggling work calls, trying to sort out job-site dramas before the first bounce. Over in the corner, one of the younger blokes is lying on the rubdown table, phone in hand, streaming Race 1 at Flemington, while three teammates hover around him, half-watching and half-yelling tips.

And then there's the forty-two-year-old club vice president, a legend in his own right, who's filling in for the reserves today. He's sitting in the corner already wrapped in ice, his hamstring clearly done for the day after the first quarter. He winces but doesn't complain. It's just part of it.

Among the chaos, a group of kids weave in and out of the rooms, wide-eyed and soaking it all in. They hang on every word and action, probably learning a new word...or ten that they shouldn't be. But they're loving it, and you know in a few years they'll be the ones pulling on the jumper, doing exactly what we're doing now.

It's messy. It's loud. It's far from perfect. But that's footy. And I'm about to give my pre-game speech. "Alright boys, listen up."

The noise died down. All eyes turned to me. I'd prepared for this speech like I was lawyer on a high-profile case. I had notes scribbled on the whiteboard behind me: opposition weaknesses, detailed matchups, strategies, contingencies. I'd dissected the opposition's game plan so thoroughly I probably could've told them what their full forward had for breakfast. I continue to waffle on about the opposition analysis...

"First up, their ruckman, number fifteen...loves to hit to the space on the left-hand side...let's take that side away from him." The room was silent. Too silent. I pressed on about the strengths and weaknesses of five or six of their best players before I finally going over our game plan. "Now, we've spoken about this all year. We give up no shit goals. No stupid risk from deep in defence. Only Sammy has got a license to take any risk that deep in defence, so get the ball in his hands. Now these are the angles we need to create from full back..." As I get a whiteboard marker out, I notice three or four guys checking their phones...Race 2 at Flemington must have just raced.

"Right, the biggest stat we will be tracking is uncontested marks. They're younger and probably quicker, so we need to keep the ball off them." I paused, expecting nods or a murmur of agreement. Just blank stares. The siren for half-time of the reserves sounds. Have I been talking for thirty minutes?

The following week, I knew I had to shake things up. The sterile, over-analytical speech wasn't going to cut it again. So, I started with something light...something to set the tone.

"Alright, Deon," I said, pointing to our full-back, "you're up. Let's hear it."

Deon grinned and launched into a joke. It was one I'd heard Billy Brownless tell the night before on Triple M radio...something about a brick, a feather, and a rose...but it had the boys in stitches. Just like that, the mood shifted. Everyone loosened up. From that day on, Deon telling a joke became a pre-game tradition, one that carried through to the day I stopped coaching.

Then I gave each line two specific focuses...two simple things to work on. And for the third focus, I let them decide.

"Backline, your turn. What's the third focus for this week?" I asked.

The players started throwing out ideas, debating among themselves. It wasn't just me talking at them anymore...they were engaged, taking ownership. I also saw a few nods. Progress.

I threw in one stat for context...something that really mattered. Not a spreadsheet of numbers, just one thing to drive the point home.

"Here's the only stat you need: last week, they scored 90% of their goals from turnovers. Their strength is their pace. Keep the ball off them. So, I'll be tracking uncontested marks more than anything else today."

And, of course, I worked in a bit of personality. A phrase here and there to keep them listening:

"Too many bears in one cave."

"Blind Freddy could have seen that."

"If you feast every day, you'll never have a feast in your life."

A bit like Robbo's nonsense he threw out, nobody really knew what I was talking about. But it was a way to keep the connection. Speeches were short enough to hold their attention but still delivered the key messages. I still couldn't stop the younger guys from checking the races...the same three or four checking their phones...but overall, the format had a lot more cut through. It wasn't perfect, but it worked. Better than the blank faces I was getting back a week earlier anyway!

In hindsight, looking back on the week before, I realised I'd failed by over-preparing. But in the grand scheme of things, that's the kind of failure I can live with...I cared enough to put in the work, even if the delivery was flatter than a three-day old beer. Sure, I got it wrong, but I'd rather fail by being too prepared than by winging it and letting the team down. It reminded me that effort matters, even if the execution misses the mark. You learn, you adapt, and you come back better the next time.

Another example is one of our supervisors. An easy-going lad, who got to his position as supervisor after only two years...not because he knew everything about painting, but when you read our core values, you could be mistaken for thinking that you were explaining him. A real work horse and someone that you never have to tell something to twice. The builders love him because he causes them no trouble, just gets on with the task, nothing will fluster him. He doesn't talk a big game, just lets his actions do the talking.

An area of growth for him was that sometimes he needed to be a bit firmer and not let the builders always tell him what to do when it affects our own productivity...finding that balance between being easy to deal with and standing up for himself. One day I got a call from a builder, all hot and bothered because our supervisor was being too demanding. Our supervisor told the builder to stop leaning tools against our finished walls and refused to work when they were cutting timber and creating a sawdust storm. Sure, he may have ruffled some feathers. He might have over-corrected;

he could have improved his communication on why he was upset with the builder... but he was chasing perfection. Failing by wanting to have the perfect finish? That's not the kind of failure that will keep me up at night.

But then... there's the other kind of failure. I remember the call like it was yesterday. My phone buzzed, and I saw the name flash up...one of our most loyal builders, someone who had been with us since the early days. I answered, expecting the usual banter or a quick update. Instead, his voice was sharp and straight to the point.

"Mate," he said, with just enough edge to make me sit up straighter, "your supervisor's just gone off his nut at our flooring guy. Full-blown spray, in front of everyone."

I took a deep breath. "What? What happened?"

"He reckons the flooring bloke scratched your freshly painted walls while laying the floorboards. Not ideal, sure. But, mate, this was something else...full public meltdown. Everyone was there. My guys, your guys. It was ugly."

I felt a bit sick. "Not on," I muttered, more to myself than to him. "I can't believe it. That's a bit out of character." I very much could believe it. I just felt a bit embarrassed that someone in our team would do that.

The builder paused, letting the weight of the situation hang in the silence. "Look," he said finally, "you've always been good to us. I get mistakes happen. But this? It's not a good look. It's not how we do things on our sites. I'm not sure we want him back here."

When the call ended, I just sat there, phone still in hand, staring at the wall. That knot in your stomach you get when something is so wrong, and you know it's on your shoulders? That was me. Not ideal? No. This was a different kind of failure. Not a harmless misstep like over-preparing a footy speech. This was a failure of culture; of the standards we worked so hard to set.

Later that day, I called the supervisor into the office. "What the hell happened?" I asked, trying to keep calm but failing to keep the edge out of my voice.

His face was defensive, arms crossed. "That bloke is a hack. Some idiot from out of town. Brand new paint job, and he doesn't give a shit about the freshly painted wall."

"Alright," I said, holding up a hand, "let's say he did scratch the walls. Does that give you the right to blow up at him in front of the whole site? Because I'm telling you now...that's not who we are. That's not we're about."

He shifted uncomfortably, still clinging to his justification. "I agree... but he messed up our work. Don't get angry at me because I care so much," he responded. Missing the point.

"And you think humiliating someone fixes that? I bet you've accidentally damaged someone's work before." He had in fact spilt some paint on the carpet a few months earlier. "You're never ever to do that again." Spoiler alert...he did do that again.

He didn't have much to say after that, just mumbled an apology. But the damage was done. That was the kind of failure that makes you want to reach for a drink. It wasn't just a bad day at work...it was a moment that went against everything I wanted this business to stand for.

We don't fail by abusing people. That's not how I want to be known. That's not who we are. This business wasn't built on shouting matches or tearing people down... relationships with clients, contractors, and everyone who crosses our path. That's our thing. And when something like this happens, it's not just a slip-up...it feels personal. It feels like a betrayal of everything we've worked so hard to create.

We can fail in so many ways. We can miss deadlines, we can get things wrong, we can lose jobs to competitors. That's life, and that's business. But this? Failing by treating someone poorly, by letting frustration boil over into something ugly and unprofessional...that's a bad way to fail. It doesn't just hurt the person on the receiving end. It hurts our team, our culture, and the relationships that are the backbone of everything we do. Even Blind Freddy could tell you that.

CHAPTER 11

WHAT IS SUCCESS, REALLY?

It's a question I've wrestled with countless times, until I heard Zoe Foster Blake frame it in a way that struck me deeply. Sure, she's not the first to have this groundbreaking epiphany, but coming from someone who appears to embody success, it hit differently. Looking in from the outside, Zoe is the picture of achievement: she sold her company for tens of millions, comes across as incredibly smart and measured, is well-travelled, writes books, and generally seems to crush it at every turn. Yet, when asked about her success, she boiled it down to something surprisingly simple and profound...wealth is time. She gave an example that stuck with me. A friend of hers had what most people would label a super successful job...a ridiculously high salary, a high-profile career. But when his dad was dying, the most important thing wasn't his title, his paycheck, or his prestige. It was the fact that he could take time off to spend every single day with his dad. That's what mattered. That's real wealth.

It made me think about the endless drive of ambitious people... entrepreneurs, managers, leaders...they're wired to move. Sitting idle feels almost unbearable. It's like there's a compulsion to fill every moment with something productive. When my life feels chaotic, my natural response isn't to slow down...it's to throw more fuel on the fire. To pile on. To keep climbing. It's a strange kind of self-inflicted frenzy. And yet, when I take the afternoon off for a round of golf or slow down to spend time with family, there's a creeping guilt. It's ridiculous, but it's real.

That's the paradox. The goal isn't to be busy all the time... it's to build something sustainable. To create a business or a career that doesn't just demand all your time but gives you time back. That should be the real aim: a business that's autonomous enough to allow you to do the things that matter. Maybe the shift isn't monumental. Maybe it's subtle. The work we do should still have purpose and ambition, but it needs to count. Every hour spent working is an hour you're not spending with family, friends, on the golf course. So, if you're going to spend that hour, make it count. Make it purposeful. That's the challenge, though, isn't it? Knowing when to stop. Knowing that success isn't just measured in milestones, sales, or hours logged at your desk. Wealth is time. And real success is having the clarity to know how to spend it.

Honestly, even if I won the lotto, I'd keep working. I thrive on challenges and sitting idle drives me crazy. But the real question is: how do you manage the balance between being too busy and too idle? Every business decision I make now starts with one guiding question: how will this make my life better?

Take outsourcing our HR, for example. Sure, it cost us a little. Our profit margins might've been a touch higher if we had kept it in-house, but you know what? It freed up hours each week and handed over the responsibility to someone better equipped for it. I'd rather have those four hours back per week in my life than an extra profit per year. Time is worth more than money. That's something I've had to learn through experience, and it's changed the way I approach every decision.

Now, I know these aren't decisions you can make straight away. When you're just starting out, you're probably hustling and learning, trying to make every minute count. I remember those days well. You don't just get to take a day off to write a book or outsource tasks because you feel like it. At the beginning, you're laying the foundation, building momentum, and keeping your head above water. But over time, as your business finds its feet and becomes more stable, there's an important mindset shift that needs to happen. It's no longer about filling every minute; it's about making the minutes count in ways that align with your values and goals.

Even writing this book started with the same question: will this make my life better? Do I have the time, and is it worth it? The answer was yes, even though I knew it would mean sacrificing other things. Writing has been something I've wanted to do forever, and while it's time-consuming, it reminded me of why I love what I do and what I need to do to stay good at it. If no one reads it, I'm okay with that. It's been worth it for me, and hopefully, it's worth something to the team...whether they learn from it or just have a laugh.

But I'll admit, this wasn't always how I thought about things. The old me would've said, "I'll just do it every night after work or block out six hours on a Saturday morning". But that's counterproductive to what I'm trying to build...a life where time isn't stolen from the people and activities I love. So instead, I shifted priorities. Writing came at the expense of a few profitable ideas I had in the pipeline or an extra day on the tools. But that's okay. Just like outsourcing HR, if it means sacrificing a bit of profit to fulfill something meaningful, I'm doing it. It all comes back to time...my most valuable currency. And like I said before, being a 'red' personality, once the idea hit me, I launched into it straight away. Old habits, hey? But this time, I think I've got a little better balance. Over time, that balance is the key to making success not just about what you've built but about how it lets you spend the moments that matter most.

Sitting Idle and Saying No to The Rodeo

When I first started my business, I was like a man possessed. I didn't say no to anything. One door to paint in Trentham? Yeah, I'll do it. Massive renovation in St Kilda at the same time as a development starting in Ballarat? Yeah I'll fit it in. Every opportunity felt like the one that could make or break me. I dove headfirst into the chaos, chasing every lead, every dollar.

I remember painting late into the night in Albert Park, three Fridays in a row. The hum of Friday night footy on the radio kept me company, along with a greasy pizza for dinner. My mates would be out having beers, laughing at the pub or at a party. Saturday, I'd let loose...work in the morning and then play catch-up socially, drink way too much, and spend Sunday trying to patch myself together. Admin work was a blur of head noise before the cycle started again Monday morning.

There wasn't a time to stop, think or breathe. The bigger picture was a luxury I couldn't afford. The tools were my safety net...they were tangible. Progress was visible: brush strokes turning into finished walls, hours turning into pay checks. But the deadlines were relentless, the pressure crushing. Take this example that summarises exactly where I was at.

Albert Park, late Friday afternoon. The site had the kind of charm you only find in places with history. The front of the building was a heritage-listed shopfront, lovingly restored to preserve every ounce of its 1930s character. Intricate cornices, leadlight windows, and weathered bricks now freshly painted but still telling their story. Behind it, though, was a completely different world – an extension that screamed modern luxury. Glass walls, sharp angles, polished concrete floors. The blend of old and new was stunning, but the job wasn't quite there yet. Almost...but not quite.

I stood in the middle of it all, brush in hand, surveying the chaos. The air smelled like sawdust and paint fumes, and the impact of a drill echoed from somewhere out the back. I glanced around. I was the last one standing, the only other guy apart from the builder still on-site late on a Friday.

The builder wandered over, his boots heavy on the timber floors. He was older, with a permanent frown etched into his face. "You nearly done here?" he asked, arms crossed, scanning the walls like a schoolteacher marking homework.

"Almost," I replied, stepping back from the feature wall I'd been working on. "Another few hours tomorrow, and I reckon I'll finish all the defects on Monday and Tuesday."

He shook his head, letting out a low chuckle that made my stomach sink. "Mate, handover's Wednesday. And I've got cleaners here early next week. You can't be leaving stuff for tomorrow. Plumbers haven't even been through to put the toilet in, the skirting boards still need fixing, and that bloody skip out front is holding up the landscapers. It's all gotta happen fast."

I frowned and looked around. He wasn't exaggerating...there was no way this job was hitting Wednesday. The skip bin still blocked the driveway, scaffold towered over the backyard, and the final clean? A pipe dream at this point.

"Yeah, but that's not really on me, is it?" I tried to keep my tone even. I wasn't in the mood for an argument. "I'm doing my part. Besides, I've got plans tomorrow night. Big weekend ahead."

The builder raised an eyebrow, leaning in like he had a secret to share. "Look, mate, you're running your own business now. That comes with sacrifices. You can't just take off whenever you want. You've gotta knuckle down if you want to succeed." I'm sure he didn't say that exactly, but my memory is that it was said in an "I'm older, I know how to manipulate you" kind of way.

I opened my mouth to argue, but he cut me off. "You don't want people saying your work held up the job, do you? That's not the kind of reputation you want. You're young, yeah, but you're running the show now. Time to step up." Again, not exact...but you get the picture. This muppet was giving me a pep talk.

I hesitated, glancing at my phone. My mate's bucks party was the next day. I'd been looking forward to it for weeks, even sacrificing a few quiet weekends to get this job done early. The carrot was so close...finish up and enjoy the night. But now? The builder's voice echoed in my head: You've gotta make sacrifices.

"Yeah, alright," I muttered, defeated. "I'll stay back tonight and put in a full day tomorrow."

The builder patted me on the shoulder. "Good lad. You'll thank me later."

Spoiler alert. I fucking did not thank him later.

By the time I hit the so-called deadline, the job wasn't even finished. The plumbers were still installing toilets, the skirting boards were half-done, and the scaffolding was still up. The landscapers hadn't even touched the garden. The deadline? A total sham. I'd caved, missed the bucks, and for what? Nothing.

And then came the next job. The next deadline. The next missed event. I was in my mid-twenties, running hard but running nowhere. Chasing someone else's schedule, someone else's expectations, and losing sight of what I wanted.

That was the moment I knew something had to change. I didn't want my life to be defined by manipulated sacrifices and missed milestones. I wanted more out of life than chasing sham deadlines for other people's benefit It was time to start running in the right direction...my direction.

Years later, the business was in a much better position. I had a crew of fifteen and growing. Deadlines? Not an issue anymore. I had the manpower to spare, systems in place, and balance...or so I thought. I was spending more work time working on the business and less time in. On paper, it looked great.

But here's the catch: the mental load never went away. The business never switched off because I never let it. Everything had to go through me. Every decision, every problem, every client issue...it was all mine. I couldn't let go. The work wasn't physical anymore, but my brain never stopped racing. Here's another buck's show story, with the comparison on where I was at this time, compared to the one I had missed years earlier. It was a day at the races, but as most of these weekends go, everyone gets excited, and the group message fires up on Friday afternoon...pub?

The Marquis of Lorne had that warm, lively buzz you only find on a Friday night. I hadn't been here in a while. Footy season had me here every Friday afternoon putting on my footy tips and having a pot. This spring night, pints clinked, laughter rolled through the room, and the smell of their legendary chicken schnitzels floated through the air. I'd knocked off work an hour ago, thrown on a clean shirt, and headed straight there. It was the perfect kick-off for what was shaping up to be a legendary weekend...a buck's party at the Cox Plate, beers, and good mates.

The first round went down easy, the kind of drink that signals you've officially clocked off. We were already swapping terrible jokes and rehashing previous buck's show stories when my phone buzzed in my pocket.

I glanced at it. A missed call. Then another buzz...this time, a message. I ignored it, shoving the phone back in my jeans. Not tonight.

By the second round, it buzzed again. Then again.

One of the boys raised an eyebrow. "You running a call centre over there, mate? Put the bloody thing away."

"Yeah," I muttered, taking a sip of my pint and pulling out my phone. "I'll just check this one."

Big mistake. I hate checking in on work when I'm trying to be social...but the unknown made it worse. It was an email from a client, furious about a job delay. A text from a contractor who'd lost some paperwork. And another missed call from someone I didn't even want to think about.

"You good?" one of the guys asked, noticing my shoulders slumping, my beer demolished.

"Yeah, all good," I lied, shoving the phone back in my pocket and forcing a smile. But my head wasn't in the pub anymore.

The next morning, the excitement of the Cox Plate couldn't even pull me out of the haze. I laced up my runners, hoping a jog would help me reset. Fitzroy Gardens was quiet, the trees swaying gently in the early breeze. I passed the MCG and Rod Laver Arena, a few run clubs around, but surprisingly quiet. By the time I hit the Yarra and made my way through the Botanic Gardens, my mind felt clearer.

For a moment, I thought I'd managed to shake it.

But as I pulled on my suit, my phone dinged again. An issue had popped up at one of our job sites. Our spray gun was having a meltdown, and the builder was wanting to know what our plan

B was...because if the boundary fences didn't get sprayed today, the world might end?

By Race 3 at the Cox Plate, I wasn't watching the horses thunder down the track. I was jugging an angry client's defect list, a quote request, and a string of calls from subcontractors who couldn't seem to find the answers themselves.

Physically, I was at the races. But I wasn't there...not really. Mentally? I was knee-deep in spreadsheets, emails, and problems I couldn't fix from a distance. I'd evolved, sure. I wasn't missing events anymore...I was showing up. But was this really any better? My body was in one place, but my head was still at work. I'd traded one kind of imbalance for another, and it was clear something still had to give.

The question wasn't just about being there anymore. It was about really being there...present, engaged, and fully off the clock. And if I couldn't figure that out, what was the point?

What is success? It's a question I've wrestled with, and the answer keeps evolving. Whatever I was doing in the past wasn't it. I'd scaled the business, built a team, and ticked off the traditional boxes of success, but it never felt quite right. People would ask, "How many workers do you have?" and the admiration would grow as the number went up. But I didn't feel any more fulfilled. The bigger the business got, the further away I felt from what truly mattered.

One key part of finding balance is figuring out what makes you happy. For me, it's taken time. In my twenties, I said yes to everything...work, social events, jobs that pushed me to the limits. "Want to come to the rodeo this weekend?" "Sure" I'd answer, barely thinking about it.

I didn't know the first thing about rodeos. I didn't own a cowboy hat, and the closest I'd ever come to riding a bull was hanging onto a mate's shoulders after one too many beers. But I said yes, because that's what my twenties were about...saying yes to everything.

ACCIDENTALLY IN CHARGE

Back then, the answer was always yes.

"Can you stay late and finish up this job?" Yes.

"Want to climb Mt Kosciusko?" Yes.

"Think you can manage this massive project even though it's way outside your skillset?" Absolutely, yes.

In hindsight, that chapter of my life was chaotic and exhausting, but it was also exactly what I needed. Those years were all about exploring, hustling, and figuring out what I liked, what I didn't, and what I could handle. It was saying yes to every opportunity, every social event, every challenge, and squeezing the juice out of every moment.

That time was all trial and error, figuring out what sticks. But now, I've realised you can't do it all. And more importantly, you don't even want to. I've gotten clarity on what matters most: travel, family and friends, golf, that second coffee from a cafe, Pilates, a swim or a run once a day, and watching the Bulldogs. That's enough for me.

So now, those things go to the top of the list. Non-negotiable. I'll splurge on a Bulldogs membership so I can sit behind the glass with friends and family for a few games. I'll play golf when the sun is out, even if it's a Tuesday morning. I'll make sure to fit in daily exercise, even when the schedule is tight. Work comes after all that because running a business means sacrifice...I know that, but those sacrifices only make sense if I've prioritised what's truly important.

Working at the co-working space of the Commons has also been a game-changer for me. It's more than just a workspace; a source of inspiration and connection. They have venues where you can work from around Melbourne and Sydney. Friday knockoffs there have become one of my favourite rituals...a release for everyone at the end of the week where I can have a drink with some of the most driven and ambitious people I've met. The energy of that community keeps me sharp, and I've learned a lot just by being around such a diverse group. The collaboration opportunities have been incredible too.

There's something special about how The Commons connects to the city I love. Whether I'm working out of Collingwood, South Melbourne, Richmond, or even South Yarra, I get to feel the pulse of each suburb. And when I'm in Sydney...Chippendale or Surrey Hills, it's the same. The spaces remind me why I love what I do and keep me grounded in the balance I'm chasing.

For me, success isn't about the size of my business or the number of jobs we take on. It's about prioritising the right things, not everything. It's the freedom to choose how I spend my time and who I spend it with. It's being able to take a weekend off and not feel guilty, to be fully present at a buck's show, without my phone pulling me away. It's about saying no to rodeos and yes to the things I love.

CHAPTER 12

THE SHINY BALL SYNDROME

You've probably heard the saying: "Cheap, quick, and quality ... you can only pick two." It's a universal truth in most industries, and it's no different in painting. When it comes to quoting jobs, we believe in applying this concept with full transparency, ensuring clients understand the trade-offs and get the value they're after.

First things first...we don't aim to be the cheapest or quickest. That's not where quality lives, and quality is where we stake our reputation. If a client is after a 'just slap a coat on it' kind of job, there are plenty of other operators who can do that for them. But that's not us. Instead, we guide clients through their options so they can make an informed choice.

We explain their options clearly:

Option A: A no-frills job that's cheaper but compromises on durability and longevity (maybe find someone else).

Option B: An ultra-premium job with every step executed to perfection, at a premium price.

Option C: A well-thought-out middle ground that balances cost and quality without cutting corners where it matters most.

This transparency is crucial because it keeps both us and the client focused on what really matters: delivering value without overpromising or cutting corners. But this approach also reflects a broader lesson I've learned in business: the danger of shiny ball syndrome.

In business, as in life, the temptation to chase the next shiny ball is ever-present. A new idea, project, or opportunity always seems exciting, full of potential and promise. But constantly chasing the next big thing...whether it's a new trend, an ambitious expansion, or a shiny new contract...can pull you off track. It spreads your focus too thin, making it impossible to fully capitalise on what's already working.

It's like running up a mountain while stopping to inspect every shiny rock along the way. Eventually, you burn out or lose sight of the summit altogether. That's why it's so important to strike the right balance between exploration and execution. Following something like Google's 80/20 rule...spending 80% of your time refining what you know works and 20% experimenting with new ideas...helps you stay focused and productive without getting distracted.

This balance is often referred to as the explore/exploit trade-off. Early on, you need to explore: test ideas, experiment, and figure out what works. But once you've found the formula, the focus should shift to exploiting it...refining, honing, and perfecting. There's always room for some experimentation to keep things dynamic, but true progress comes from mastering the basics and doubling down on what works. It's about being flexible, but not reactive.

This idea has guided many decisions in our business, especially as we've grown. Growth isn't about expanding every part of the company all at once...it's about knowing when to slow down in one area so another can thrive. For example, when we began transitioning some of our best painters into leadership roles, I thought the best painter would naturally make the best supervisor. It seemed logical.

But I quickly learned that leadership requires a completely different skill set. The technical ability that makes someone a standout on the tools doesn't necessarily make them a great leader. Leadership demands patience, communication, and the ability to foster growth in others. It's a different mountain to climb, and just like any new journey, you don't start at the top simply because you excelled in your previous role.

Promoting leaders now is a more deliberate process. We focus on attitude, values, and the ability to inspire and guide a team. True growth means balancing ambition with patience...moving fast enough to stay motivated but slow enough to make it sustainable.

In painting, as in business, mastery comes from repetition and refinement. The best athletes and musicians understand this. Think of the 10,000-hour rule made famous by Malcolm Gladwell...it's the idea that true expertise comes from hours upon hours of deliberate practice. Repetition isn't sexy. It's not flashy. It's just showing up, day after day, and doing the work. But here's the catch: it's not just repetition for repetition's sake. It's repeating what works.

For us, painting office spaces works. They've become our bread and butter. We've built a skilled crew that knows how to get in and out quickly without disrupting the business day. They don't have the complexities of new builds...fewer trades to navigate, fewer surprises. They're profitable, efficient, and often in great locations around Melbourne. Many a time I've seen my workers perched up at The Commons bar, enjoying a beer after finishing a job, and I get it...those projects have an energy about them that everyone loves.

So, we exploit that. Whenever a request comes through for an office space, it's priority number one. It's where we focus our marketing. It's what we've refined to a science, and we make sure to keep it our number one priority.

But here's the thing: while repetition and exploitation of what works are key, there's always a need for that 20%...the room for innovation. Like I explained in an earlier chapter, you need people wearing different hats, offering fresh ideas, and exploring the next big thing. Maybe it's carving out a specific time of the week when you or your team can focus on creativity, or putting someone with a curious, innovative mindset in charge of finding the next "office space win".

You can't afford to let your business...or your thinking...go stale. Whether it's projects, processes, or strategies that have worked forever, there's always an opportunity to ask: "Is there a better way to do this?" Repetition is the foundation of mastery, but innovation is the spark that keeps it alive.

So, yes, we'll continue to prioritise office spaces because they work, but we'll also keep that 20% for experimentation...because one day, we might find something that works even better.

Mastery is about doing the fundamentals better than anyone else, but true greatness is found in striking the balance between exploiting what works and staying open to the possibility of what could.

Business Lunch or Reverse Raffle?

Business lunches are a strange beast...equal parts networking opportunity, keynote speakers, and socially acceptable daytime drinking. I get invites every so often, often through Dulux and their partnership with the Geelong Football Club. On the surface, it's a chance to rub shoulders with local businesses (which I find awkward), soak up some wisdom from sports and business leaders, and, let's be honest, enjoy some free beer and food. But the value of these events goes far deeper than that.

Just on referring to myself as being awkward with networking, it made me think about why this is. Traditional networking has never been my thing. The idea of walking into a room full of strangers, striking up conversations, and "rubbing shoulders" with other business owners is daunting to me. I'm naturally quite shy at these kinds of events, and I've never been the type to take charge and initiate conversations without knowing someone first.

That's why I've grown to love The Commons. It's a coworking space full of stimulating, inspiring people, and while it took me a while to feel comfortable there, it's become one of my favourite places to be. At first, I was the guy quietly going about my business, avoiding too much interaction. But as time passed, I started to feel at ease. Now, I'm always pestering people, asking questions, and soaking up what I can learn from them. It's amazing. But those traditional, suit-and-tie networking events? They're still a struggle.

I've always thought of myself as an introvert, and I remember having a conversation with someone at The Commons about this. "I guess I'm the type of person who likes to go unnoticed, hates being the centre of attention...definitely an introvert," I said.

"No, you're not," she responded immediately.

"Well, I think I am. It's just that I've been here a while now, and I'm more comfortable."

"Why is that? Let's unpack that."

"No thank you. Let's talk about someone else," I deflected.

"Would you send your food back if you got a bad meal?"

"No way. I wouldn't send it back if it had a band-aid in it."

And so, it went on. She wasn't convinced that I was truly introverted and instead pointed me toward a podcast by Zoe Foster Blake. "She explains it better than I can," she said, admittedly after a couple too many gins. "You need to listen to how she articulates this… it'll resonate with you."

Now, I've always loved listening to Zoe Foster Blake, so I didn't need much encouragement. And she absolutely nailed it. In the podcast, she described herself as an introvert, which I found surprising at first. But then she explained it in a way that clicked with me: "*I realised I'm not an introvert. I just get introverted hangovers. I can perform in front of people and be great for a few hours a night maybe, but the next day… I'm zonked.*"

That resonated deeply with me. I don't mind being social in short bursts…I can be social when I need to. But afterwards, I need to recharge. She went on to explain the different types of communicators, which gave me even more clarity. "*You can be someone like my husband (Hamish Blake), who is extroverted and a skilled communicator. Or you can be a skilled communicator who is introverted (which is what she labelled herself). Then there are poor communicators and introverted, which makes it hard to be social. And the worst type,*" she said with a laugh, "*are extroverts with no social skills…AKA the dickheads.*"

That podcast gave me a new way to think about myself and how I interact with others. I'm not the life of the party, but I can connect when I feel comfortable. I just need to recharge afterward. And that's okay.

When it comes to professional development and networking, I've found ways to work with my nature instead of against it. I still struggle with traditional networking events, but I try to go, especially when Dulux or other partners invite me to lunches or workshops. I've also made it a priority to organise personal development opportunities for my crew. Whether it's attending leadership courses, trade events, or Dulux workshops, I want to give everyone on the team a chance to learn and grow.

Sometimes these events give you a sugar hit of motivation that lasts a few days. Other times, something more profound sticks with you for months, years, or even forever. And even if the takeaway isn't earth-shattering, it's always a chance to break the routine, come back fresh, and learn something new. Plus, as I like to remind myself, there's almost always a beer waiting at the end of it. Anyway, I've gone off course a little there. Back to the actual story.

This time the event was The Resilience Project, and the speaker wasn't Hugh Van Cuylenberg, whose books I've devoured and gratitude diaries I've scribbled into. No, it was Martin Heppel...a name I'd heard in passing but knew little about.

Intrigued, I booked a table of ten and invited our supervisors...a motley crew of mostly young guys, who were, let's just say, unfamiliar with the finer points of a business lunch – as I had been a few years earlier when I treated it like a reverse raffle at your local footy club and had too many pints. Their interpretation of 'business casual' was nothing short of spectacular. One guy showed up in a suit so loose it looked like he borrowed it from his dad. Another rocked a shirt that technically had a collar but had seen better days. And then there were the wildcard attendees, who's ideal of 'casual' teetered closer to backyard BBQ.

When we arrived, it was clear where the riffraff belonged: the painters were sent to the back of the room. The mood was set...live acoustic guitar, the gentle hum of chatter, and the steady clinking of champagne flutes. The crew wasted no time. Within minutes, someone had swapped name tags with a stranger for laughs. He thought it was the funniest thing since Seinfeld. The waiter found himself running an official shuttle service between our table and the bar. The poor bloke was sweating bullets, but to his credit, he kept pace. The first speaker was an economist, armed with slides and graphs detailing the financial impact of a Geelong home game. It was death by PowerPoint. He droned about ticket sales, tourism dollars, and some multiplier effects I didn't bother to understand. Our table? Unfazed. One guy was doing an impression of the speaker mid-graph. Our Kiwi supervisor was making regular pilgrimages to the smoking area, clocking up more km's than the bar staff. When he came back, he proudly announced he'd made a cameo on Channel Nine news, standing in the background, chain smoking, as Geelong's latest recruit, Bailey Smith, strolled past. "Some blonde guy with a mullet just walked in with a camera crew in tow," he proudly declared. He was, in fact, on the news later that night.

Then came the CEO of Marathon Foods, the company behind the dim sims served at Geelong home games. Now, I love a dim sim as much as the next person, but nothing prepared me for the sheer, unbridled chaos that erupted at our table. It was as if dim sims were the cornerstone of life itself. Or maybe the booze was kicking in... scratch that, it was definitely the booze.

As the dim sim CEO slowly spoke, he laboured over how much the partnership between Marathon and Geelong Football Club meant to him and how important it truly was...one of our crew, eyes slightly glazed and grin wide, suddenly leapt to his feet. He clapped wildly, a thunderous standing ovation that echoed through the room. "Dim sims! Let's actually go!" he bellowed, voice breaking with what can only be described as drunken nonsense.

The rest of the table, not to be outdone, joined in like a rogue football crowd. People were pounding on the table, spilling beer and sloshing wine in the process. "Yeah! Dim sims!" someone else shouted, while others whistled and hollered as if the CEO had just delivered the Gettysburg Address.

The poor CEO stood there, blinking in stunned silence, caught somewhere between flattery and sheer confusion. He smiled politely, raising a hand in acknowledgment like a reluctant rock star dragged on stage for an encore.

Meanwhile, I was trying to become one with my chair, silently debating whether crawling under the table was an appropriate move. But despite my mortification, I couldn't stop laughing. The absurdity of the moment...the clapping, the hollering, the sheer commitment to dim sim worship...was too much. It was chaos. Pure, ridiculous chaos.

By the time Martin Heppell took the stage, the room was primed, with our crew having already switched to cocktails. Martin hit the ground running with an intensity that made even our rowdy lot sit up. For the first two minutes, I wasn't sold. He was loud, almost confrontational, as I whispered to the waiter, "I'll get involved in them cocktails please". Might as well get our money's worth. But then, something shifted. His passion cut through the noise, and the room, our table included...fell silent. Even the waiter, perhaps sensing the shift in energy, gave us a momentary reprieve.

Martin's message was simple but powerful. "You're all so busy chasing more," he began, pacing the stage like a man possessed. "You work your asses off for a dream holiday house, across the bay, maybe in Rye, with an outdoor shower. You're on Realestate. com every night. It's a little out of reach, but if you grind a little harder, you'll get there. And you do. And when you finally get it, you're happy...for a moment."

He paused, letting the room squirm. "Then you meet someone with a place near The Conti in Sorrento, and they invite you out for tea. You're having a great night, and you think, how good would it be to walk home after a bottle of wine? Way better than having to order a cab. So, you grind harder, you're back on Realestate.com. You now want this more than anything in your life. And again, you get there. You upgrade, and for a while, you're happy again. And then you're out for lunch with your new flash friends at the Conti, and you better believe it...you're having a few bottles of wine...because you can walk home from here! You look around and laugh at the shmucks that have to catch a cab. And that's when you see it... a helicopter flying overhead... and it's Linsday Fox flying home to his place in Portsea! And you think, that'd be nice, something a little more private...and the cycle starts over."

It was like being hit by a freight train. His words weren't just an observation...they were a mirror. I looked around the room...and I reckon there were a few mirrors getting held up.

And then he drove it home. "Success isn't about more. It's about knowing when to stop. Knowing what's enough."

For me, it hit close to home. Not long ago, Edwina and I bought an apartment in Collingwood...my dream spot. We'd walk across Gertrude Street, smelling the coffee from Burnside, Archies and many more cafes. We'd turn down Napier St, past the Union, Napier Hotel and The Rose that lived on the corners of tree-lined beautiful streets, soaking in the life we built. But already, as we walked further north up Napier St, I'd started fantasising about something bigger...a place with more north facing sun, closer to Edinburgh Gardens, perhaps? Hearing Martin's words, I realised how ridiculous that was. Appreciate what you got. Smell the roses. I realised how true it was. Our apartment just off Smith Street, with Edwina by my side, that was perfect. If you spend your whole life chasing, hustling, wanting more, you'll never be satisfied.

THE SHINY BALL SYNDROME

By the end of Martin's talk, my team was back to their antics, but I was somewhere else entirely. His intensity, his message...it shook me in the best way possible. Maybe this wasn't just another business lunch after all. Maybe it was exactly what I needed to hear.

CHAPTER 13

PRACTICE OVER PLANNING

The most effective form of learning isn't rooted in endless planning or perfect strategies...it's about getting your hands dirty and learning through doing. I've always believed in this philosophy... strategy is important, no doubt. Pat Cummins once said that to succeed, you need a vision, and that vision must be exciting. He's right. You need something to aim for, something that gives your work meaning. But here's the key...don't over-strategise at the expense of action. Vision is crucial, but you won't get anywhere without execution. You learn on the go, and often, the best insights come from experience rather than theory.

A powerful example of this comes from a photography class explained by Steven Bartlett. The class was divided into two groups: one spent three months meticulously planning the perfect photo. They mapped out every detail – the best lighting, weather, model placement, timing. The other group took a different approach...

they started taking photos straight away, learning by trial and error, adjusting their techniques as they went.

At the end of the experiment, something interesting happened. Despite the planning group having a detailed strategy and a clear vision, the group that focused on practice and learning by doing produced better results. The group that embraced trial and error didn't just improve; they evolved more quickly, adapting their approach based on the immediate feedback they received from each shot. Their progress came from adjusting their approach along the way, honing their skills in real-time.

This underscores an important lesson: while strategy and planning have their place, real growth happens when you act and refine as you go. The hands-on experience provides immediate feedback, helping you adjust and improve far more effectively than static planning ever could. It's about diving in, taking those initial missteps, and learning on the fly.

This principle applies to everything in business. You can map out the perfect plan for hiring, marketing, or operational efficiency, but the reality is, things rarely go exactly to plan. That's why having the right people in the right roles is more important than any rigid strategy. In future chapters, I'll talk about the importance of building a team that can adapt – because when things inevitably take an unexpected turn, the people steering the ship matter more than the original route.

Phil Jackson, the legendary basketball coach, once said, *"Like most things in life, the best approach is always the simplest"*. It's the same principle here...know your business, have an exciting vision, surround yourself with the right people who can navigate challenges, but most importantly, just get into it. Start, learn, adjust, and keep moving forward.

I've seen too many people get stuck in the trap of waiting for the perfect moment. But the truth is, the perfect moment never comes.

The real magic happens when you start...when you stop hesitating, act, and refine your approach in real time. The most successful people aren't the ones with the most detailed plans; they're the ones who take imperfect action and course-correct along the way.

And this doesn't just apply to business. I've seen it in life, repeatedly. I won't go travelling this year because my footy team is going well, and I don't want to miss out on winning a premiership. I won't take an RDO because work is too busy. I won't go on this date because I don't like their tattoos. These things seem valid at the time, but the reality is, if you go looking for a reason not to do something, you'll always find one. There will always be an excuse...a reason to put something off, to delay, to wait for that perfect set of conditions that never actually arrives.

The problem is, while you're waiting, life keeps moving. Time doesn't pause for you to feel completely ready. Opportunities don't sit around waiting for you to be comfortable enough to take them. Life rewards action.

Some of the best things that have ever happened to me, personally and in business...came from simply saying yes before I had everything figured out. Booking the trip before I knew how it would all work. Taking the meeting before I felt fully prepared. Hiring someone before I had the perfect role lined up. Deciding and backing myself, trusting that I'd figure it out along the way.

Because here's the thing: nobody ever feels completely ready. Everyone is making it up as they go, to some degree. And the people who get ahead, the ones who make the most of their opportunities, are the ones who act despite that uncertainty. They move first and adjust as they go.

I'm not saying you should be reckless or throw yourself into things blindly. But I am saying that waiting for the stars to align, for the timing to be just right, often means waiting forever. You'll never feel perfectly ready to start that business, change careers, move cities, or take that leap in life. And yet, if you trust yourself to learn and adapt along the way, you'll look back and realise that starting was the most important thing you ever did.

So don't overthink it. Say yes. Take the RDO. Book the trip. Go on the date. Stop waiting for life to hand you the perfect conditions and start making the most of the ones you have. Because the only way to truly move forward is to start walking. So, whatever it is – business, leadership, personal growth...get moving. Learn on the run. See what works and improve from there. Because practice isn't just the key to mastery; it's the only way to truly evolve.

Getting Scammed Along the Way

I was six weeks into a South American adventure, halfway to nowhere on Ilha Grande, a remote island off the coast of Brazil where the beaches looked like something straight out of a dream. The sunsets were surreal...melting into turquoise waters, casting golden shadows over jungle-covered hills. Ilha Grande had everything... swaying palm trees, stretches of untouched sand, a vibe so laid-back it could make anyone forget reality. The only snag? It was a cash-only paradise. No cards, no apps, just good old Brazilian reals.

We didn't know this until we got there. We'd arrived by ferry, backpacks slung over our shoulders, stepping onto what felt like a hidden utopia. But within minutes, the realisation hit...no one would accept a bank card. This was in 2015 too, not fifty years ago, but nobody accepted card! Not the beachside stalls selling fresh coconuts, not the tiny family-run pousadas, not even the places renting out snorkels or surfboards. No cash, no luck. And us? Barely a single real between us.

The first day was spent scraping by. Between the three of us we had a small amount of Brazilian real, Aussie money, and some left over

US dollars and stretched every cent we could scavenge. We needed an ATM, and fast. But this was an island built for escaping modern life. There were no banks, no proper financial infrastructure...just whispered rumours of a single ATM hidden somewhere deep in the village.

And that's when we met *him*. A local, appearing out of nowhere like he'd been sent by the universe, claiming he knew exactly where we could withdraw cash. Desperate, we followed.

The further we walked, the dodgier it got. We weaved through back alleys, dodging stray dogs and stepping over cracked cobblestones. The air smelled of salt and grilled fish from a nearby market. The deeper in we went, the more I felt that creeping "are we about to be in a Netflix documentary?" kind of feeling.

Finally, we stopped in front of a lone ATM tucked into a dark alcove, flickering under a single buzzing light. It had all the charm of a backroom poker den. The kind of place where you might withdraw cash only to find out later, you'd just bought a second-hand boat without knowing it.

"Tem dinheiro aqui," the guy said, grinning.

We hesitated. But we were desperate. We slid in our cards, typed our pins, and took out as much as we could. Our guide nodded, looking almost too pleased. We thanked him, stuffed our pockets with cash, and walked back into the sun like kings.

And man, did we enjoy it.

We spent the day soaking up Ilha Grande properly. First stop – a run through the jungle to Lopes Mendes, a beach so stunning it had been voted the best in the world. The track wound through thick rainforest, the air humid and alive with the sounds of unseen creatures rustling in the trees. Leaves crunched underfoot, the earthy smell of damp soil filling our lungs. Sunlight filtered through the trees in dappled patches as we jogged past vines and towering palms. We'd come prepared...backpacks stuffed with bananas, a treat for the monkeys we'd heard about along the way. Sure enough, as we stopped for water, they appeared. Tiny, wide-eyed, and fearless. They leapt between branches, eyeing us with mischievous curiosity before snatching bananas from our hands and disappearing just as fast.

When we finally reached Lopes Mendes, it was worth it. The sand was soft and white, the waves rolling in gently like something off a postcard. We collapsed onto the shore, sweat mixing with saltwater as we dove into the water. Afterwards, we lay back in beach chairs, sipping piña coladas as the sun dipped lower, the sky turning hues of orange and pink. If paradise had a manual, this was it.

But paradise didn't last.

The high evaporated about ten minutes after we got back to town. Luke was the first to notice. He pulled out his phone, squinting at his banking app. His face dropped.

"Mate," he said, voice flat. "My card's just been rinsed."

I checked mine. Same deal. The ATM hadn't just dispensed cash... it had skimmed our details and was still bleeding our accounts dry.

Panic hit. We both started scrambling, refreshing our banking apps, watching helplessly as transactions from God-knows-where in Brazil drained our funds.

"How much?" I asked.

Luke exhaled through his teeth. "All of it, mate. Every cent I just pulled out and more."

We stood there, stunned. The noise of the island suddenly felt louder...the chatter of market vendors, the clink of beer bottles, the distant reggaeton pumping from a beachside bar. It all felt like background noise to a scene we didn't want to be in.

"The police?" I suggested.

We found them. They laughed. Actually laughed. Like a couple of clueless gringos getting scammed was the highlight of their day. One of them even slapped Luke on the back like we were old footy mates.

"Bem-vindos ao Brasil," one of them chuckled.

So, naturally, we went to confront the guy who led us there.

The conversation started in English.

"Hey, mate. That ATM scammed us."

The guy blinked. "Não entendo..."

Luke frowned. "What do you mean? You spoke perfect English before."

"Não...falo...inglês," he repeated, shaking his head dramatically, his eyes darting to the side.

Luke's jaw clenched. "Oh, you don't speak English now? Convenient."

I pulled out Google Translate on my phone. Typed in: The ATM scammed us. You led us there. Fix it.

He read it. He sighed. Then, in crystal-clear English, he suddenly found his words again.

"Okay, okay. Yes, maybe...small problem."

Luke raised an eyebrow. "Small problem? Mate, I'm watching my bank account get mugged in real-time."

The guy scratched his head. "I have solution."

Oh, this was going to be good.

"I can send money through Western Union," he said. "Or... my friend, he lives in Sydney. He play basketball. He give you money when you go home."

Luke and I just stared. I could almost hear the static in our brains.

"That's your solution?" I asked.

He nodded, dead serious.

Luke rubbed his temples. "So just to be clear... your grand plan is for us to fly home to Australia and meet your mystery mate who may or may not exist, and he'll just hand us back our money?"

The guy nodded again, smiling like he'd just cracked the Da Vinci code.

We burst out laughing. What else could we do?

We cut our losses, pooled together what money we had, bought a couple of beers, and toasted to another one of those only in Brazil stories.

The timing wasn't great. I was meant to be back in Australia soon, kicking off my new business after slogging through a part-time business diploma at RMIT. Not that I'd learned much...if I was honest, I'd signed up more for the student card and the $2 pots at Turf Bar than the actual classes.

But after Brazil, sitting in night lectures and learning from textbooks felt like a slog. That shady ATM had taught me more about the real world than any business theory ever could. I'd learned the hard way: you don't wait for the perfect conditions, you navigate through chaos, make decisions, and adjust on the fly.

I never went back to that diploma. Not because education isn't important, but because, for me, the real learning happened out there. In the mess. In the mistakes. In figuring things out the hard way.

And yeah, sometimes that means getting scammed in the middle of a Brazilian paradise.

CHAPTER 14

END OF TRIM ROUTINE

The End of Trim Routine is a brilliant concept explained in the book, *Diary of a CEO*, for anyone in a service business. Picture this: in a psychology experiment, a hairdresser gave one hundred haircuts. For the first fifty customers, he ended abruptly, skipping any extra flourishes. For the other fifty, he added an extra twenty seconds to do a fake trim, circling the client's head as if meticulously double-checking his work. The result? Customer satisfaction shot up in the second group, even though the haircut itself hadn't changed. Those last twenty seconds gave customers the reassurance that they'd received top-quality service.

Painting is remarkably similar. We could do flawless work all job long, but the client is likely to remember two things most clearly: the highlight of the project (whether good or bad) and how it ended. A fantastic paint job can be overshadowed by the smallest of details... like leaving a paint tin unlabelled, forgetting a small touch up, or neglecting to have one final walk through with them. These final moments become lasting impressions, just like the hairdressers end of trim routine.

I've seen firsthand how a strong finish...or a bad one, can shape the way people remember a job. I had a shed built at my home once. There were a few little hiccups along the way, but nothing major...nothing I hadn't seen before. And to their credit, everything got fixed. But the day they finished, it was pouring rain, and they dragged so much mud through the shed that it looked more like a dairy farm than a brand-new workspace. That's how I remember them. Not the quality of the build, not their problem-solving, just the fact that they handed over a filthy mess and walked away. I wouldn't use them again.

Then there was the time we sold our house. The whole process was great...we liked our agent, we got the price we wanted, and everything ran smoothly. But right at the end, a bunch of hidden fees were thrown at us. It left a bitter taste. That's all I remember now. Not the good service, not the great result...just the sting of feeling like we'd been blindsided at the last minute.

On the flip side, I had a tiler do some work on our house – our bathroom and splash back. It was a cashie job for him, so I wasn't expecting it to be done at lightning speed, and yeah, it did drag out a bit. But here's what I remember: at the very end, he made sure I was happy with everything. He walked me through the finished job, showed me what to do with the leftover tiles and grout, and even offered to caulk them himself, even though he knew the caulker would normally handle that part. That little extra effort, that final touch of care, stuck with me. He left me with a great impression, and I wouldn't hesitate to recommend him.

I've seen this happen in painting time and time again. By the time we get to the job, sometimes it's already over budget or past deadline. The client is exhausted. Conversations about extra costs that might have been reasonable at the start of the job, when the bricklayers or framers were still working...become far more tense when they're dealing with us. By the end, mistakes or delays that might have been brushed off earlier in the project can suddenly feel like the last straw for the client. The painters often cop the frustration of everything that's gone wrong before we even got there. It can be death by a thousand cuts.

That's why our End of Trim Routine is critical. It's our last chance to leave on a good note. That twenty-minute checklist...checking windows and door furniture for paint spots, labelling leftover tins, staining door thresholds can turn a good job into a great experience for the client. Just like the hairdresser's fake trim, that final moment of care can make all the difference in how we're remembered.

Because the truth is, problems can come up in any job. Some things are out of your control. But what is in your control is how you leave the client feeling at the very end. A strong finish isn't just about closing out the job...it's about cementing your reputation, setting up repeat business, and ensuring that when that client talks about you down the track, the story they tell is a good one.

A Man's Kerb Is His Castle

Here's a little piece of advice no one asks for, but everyone needs... in the game of reputation, the scales are wildly unbalanced. Do a great job and your client may tell five people about it. Make a mistake? Your disgruntled client will be telling anyone with ears about your supposed shortcomings. That's the deal...you're judged more harshly on your missteps than you'll ever be celebrated for your wins. Case in point is the following story...

It was a perfect winter's afternoon...sun shining, not a breath of wind, one of those days that tricks you into thinking life is smooth sailing. I parked my car outside my mate Collo's neighbour's house and hopped into his car for footy training. No big deal. Or so I thought.

Fast forward an hour, and my phone starts vibrating in my bag like it's trying to escape. Unknown number. I ignore it. It rings again. And again. Alright, alright. I answer.

"YOU THINK YOU CAN JUST PARK WHEREVER YOU BLOODY WANT?! COME AND GET YOUR FUCKING TRUCK OFF MY LAWN YOU FUCKING CUNT!"

The voice on the other end is pure rage. No warm-up, no introduction...just straight into full-volume fury. I yank the phone away from my ear, but even at arm's length, he's still blaring like a siren.

"What? Who is this?" I manage, caught completely off guard as I'm tying up my shoelaces on my footy boots.

"WHO IS THIS? WHO IS THIS? IT'S THE BLOKE WHOSE DRIVEWAY YOU'VE BLOCKED! GET YOUR FUCKING SHIT CAR OFF MY LAWN!"

I'm rattled. My car's nowhere near his driveway. Then it clicks...my front tyre, hanging over his kerb by maybe two centimetres. It's a court with a semi-circle end, that makes it hard not to have a piece of tyre on a curb...either that or your car sticks out a bit. And my stupid phone number is on my car (something I've changed since).

As I'm coming up with something to say...he hangs up.

For the next fifteen minutes I'm coming up with sledges that I should have gone back with. But the absurdity of the entire situation has thrown me.

Training was easy...short, sharp kicking drills and a few shots on goal. In between drills, I jogged over to Collo, still shaking my head at the phone call.

"Mate, you won't believe who just rang me."

He wipes sweat off his forehead. "Who?"

"Your neighbour."

END OF TRIM ROUTINE

Collo squints at me, confused. "Which one?"

"The real fun one in the single-story house."

His face twists in disbelief. "What does he want?"

"I don't know, apparently my car's ruined his life because my tyre's two centimetres over his kerb."

Collo barks out a laugh. "Jesus Christ. What, did you park it in his bloody living room?"

"I'm starting to wonder."

Nothing more needed to be said...we both knew exactly the type of bloke we were dealing with. Collo shook his head and jogged off for the next drill, but I could tell he wasn't done with this conversation.

Fifteen minutes before training was officially over, I hear his voice ring yelling to the coach, "Oi, I'm off!"

I glance over at the change rooms twenty minutes later. Collo is already showered, dressed, and looking fresh while the rest of us are still gasping through the final few drills. Of course. Classic Collo...always the first to finish up and sneak off for a massage.

I jog over. "What's up?"

His expression is different now...serious. He holds up his phone. "Rach just rang me. The neighbour's been round at ours, losing his shit at her."

My stomach tightens. "You're joking."

"Wish I was."

ACCIDENTALLY IN CHARGE

By the time training wrapped up and I'd showered, I jumped in the car with Collo, and my brain started second-guessing everything. Did I park in his bloody lounge room? Did I somehow crush his rose garden? Did I accidentally dump a tray full of asbestos on his front lawn? Why is this bloke so unhinged?

Collo, on the other hand, was fuming.

"Mate, this isn't even the worst of it," he said, gripping the steering wheel tight. "He abused my brother once for parking his trailer out front. Now he lines up all four of his cars on the street just so nobody can park out the front of his place."

I shake my head. "Sounds like a barrel of laughs this bloke."

"Oh, it gets better," Collo continues. "One night Rach and I got home from dinner, and this flog came outside just to say, 'Surprise, surprise, been out again'. Like, what the fuck is that supposed to mean?"

I let out a low whistle. "Bloke sounds like he's got nothing else going on in life."

"Nothing. Absolutely nothing."

By the time we pulled up out front, our frustration had fully brewed into let's-go-knock-on-his-door levels of anger. But Collo and Rach had to live next to this human migraine. And Rach wisely told us not to.

So, we stepped outside and went to inspect the crime scene.

There it was...my tyre, barely kissing the edge of his lawn. The nature strip, which wasn't even his, had about as much damage as a blade of grass bending in the wind.

And with that, we left it. Not because he was right. Not because we were over it. But because some people are just built to be miserable. But the story doesn't end there. Oh no, this guy wasn't content with a verbal takedown. He took his outrage to Google, slapping my business with a 1-star review. One tyre, one centimetre, one star. Suddenly, I'm not just a mildly annoying parker. I'm the villain of his suburban soap opera.

Here's the kicker...no one ever writes a glowing review saying, "Parked beautifully outside my house, disrupted absolutely nobody, 5 stars". Nope, that's not how people work. Perfection is expected and uncelebrated, but step one centimetre out of line (or over the kerb) ...it's the social equivalent of setting off a car alarm at 3am... everyone hears about it.

The takeaway? There are no small sins in the court of public opinion. Screw up once, and your mistake will get passed around like juicy gossip at a backyard barbeque. Do something great? Maybe it'll get a passing mention...if you're lucky.

Such is life in the suburbs, where every driveway is sacred, and the smallest misstep can make you a legend for all the wrong reasons. So, if you value your sanity and your Google reviews...park carefully. Because in a world like this, even a couple of centimetres can make or break you.

I Wasn't the Only 1-Star Review Off Ian (I looked up the Google reviews he had given)

Horrible experience from start to finish. $5000 wasted on a door that isn't sealing and letting in wind and rain. The owner of the business couldn't care less. I recently bought my fifth new bike from them and couldn't be more disappointed. On arriving home with my bike, I noticed major damage to the bike. The owner of the business couldn't have cared less. Once they have your money, *they close the doors. What was once a great bike shop has gone to the dogs.*

Dropped my van off for a service. Collected it later that day and the whole underside and tyres were caked with mud. No idea what they were doing with the van. When I opened the door there was a dirty wet cloth lying on the passenger seat (seat was also wet). I dread to think of some neanderthal wiping down my van with it. Not a company I would trust.

Claim to beat any advertised price but on the 8th of July 2021, the rude lady on the checkout argued that First Choice Liquor couldn't sell a slab for that price even after I showed her their website. She dug in her heels and continued to be argumentative even with a queue of customers waiting to be served. Needless to say, I happily drove to First Choice Liquor, so I didn't have to pay an over-inflated price for a slab.

CHAPTER 15

THE FOUR P'S

The four P's...Preparation Prevents Poor Performance. Not to be confused with the three P's my senior cricket club, Colac West, embraced every Thursday night after training when I was just a junior...Porn, Poker and Pizza.

In both business and sports, the concept of marginal gains has become a game-changing strategy for achieving extraordinary results. The idea is simple...by sweating the small stuff, those seemingly insignificant details, you can create a cumulative effect that drives massive improvements. It's not about revolutionary overhauls or dramatic transformations. It's about the small, consistent adjustments that, when added together, produce powerful outcomes.

Take sport for example. The British cycling team, under the leadership of Sir Dave Brailsford, became a poster boy for marginal gains. By focusing on tiny improvements...like optimising bike seats for comfort, adjusting clothing for aerodynamics, and even teaching athletes better hand-washing techniques to avoid illness...they achieved unprecedented success. They didn't try to revolutionise the sport...they made small changes, which while unimpressive on their own, added up to an unbeatable edge.

Similarly, golfer Bryson DeChambeau demonstrates this attention to detail by soaking his golf balls in Epsom salt to ensure perfect balance. It's the relentless pursuit of precision and incremental improvements that transfer good into great. And while I'm sure if I went home, filled a bucket with Epsom salt, and soaked my own golf balls, I wouldn't suddenly win the US Open...or even the Queenscliff Club Championship...it's not about the act itself. It's about what the act represents...preparation, belief and the mental edge. Standing on the first tee, the confidence Bryson must feel is profound. He's done the work. He's gone further than anyone else would. That belief, "I bet my opponents haven't gone as far as I have; I'm more prepared than the guy standing next to me" gives him a psychological edge before the game even begins.

The same principle applies to business. Fine-tuning processes, improving communication, and refining customer experience might seem like small moves, but over time, they can define whether a business thrives or merely survives. A slight improvement in email response times, a marginally better product, or even a smoother onboarding process for new employees can build a foundation for long-term success.

Why are marginal gains so impactful? Firstly, they create tangible improvements. Even if each adjustment seems insignificant, the sum of these parts can dramatically enhance performance. For example, improving efficiency by 1% in ten areas doesn't add up... it multiplies, creating exponential growth.

But beyond the numbers, marginal gains cultivate something even more valuable – confidence. When you've paid attention to the small details, you're not just better prepared...you know you're better prepared. This sense of readiness and control fosters a belief that you've left no stone unturned, that you're equipped as possible to face challenges. Confidence isn't just a byproduct of success...it's a catalyst for it.

For me confidence has a ways been rooted in my preparation. Whether I'm submitting a monster quote, hiring a team member, a making a big decision, I rely on the belief that I've done the work. I've pored over the details. analysed every angle, and left no room for doubt in my preparations. That belief...whether entirely accurate or not, is what gives me the confidence to make bold decisions.

In business I tell myself I've worked harder and analysed more thoroughly than anyone else, especially my competition. Deep down, I know that might not be true, there's always someone out there grinding just as hard. But that belief is what matters. Confidence in preparation is a self-fulfilling prophecy...the harder I work, the more confident I become.

The connection between preparation and confidence is undeniable. When you know you've done the groundwork, you free yourself from second-guessing. That clarity allows you to focus on execution instead of hesitation. Confidence, even if partially imagined, becomes a powerful tool. It's not about arrogance or pretending you have all the answers, it's about trusting that you've done everything possible to set yourself up for success.

However, the focus on marginal gains doesn't mean obsessing over irrelevant detail at the expense of the bigger picture...it's about balance. Knowing that while big picture strategy sets your directions, it's the fine-tuning of details that ensures you stay on course.

I admire how Toyota exemplifies a culture where no idea is too small. Their philosophy ensures that every suggestion is given a fair chance-provided it's accompanied by a solution. With some coaching, an impressive 99% of these ideas are implemented successfully, showing the power of a bottom-up approach.

The bottom-up approach, while incredibly powerful, isn't without its risks. When you empower the crew to contribute ideas, you're inviting them into the decision-making process...a space they might not always have the full context for. They may not be privy to executive meetings, strategic decisions, or the bigger picture that drives the company forward. As a result, some suggestions can feel off the mark or misguided at first glance. But here's the thing: that doesn't make their input any less valuable.

The key to getting the bottom-up approach right is coaching. When a suggestion comes in that doesn't align perfectly with the bigger picture, it's easy to dismiss it outright...but that's a mistake. Instead, take the time to understand the thought behind it. Often, the crew has their ear to the ground. They're living the day-to-day realities of operations, interacting with customers, and navigating the nuances of the job in ways that higher-ups may not. Their perspective is rooted in the frontline experience, and that makes their insights invaluable.

Sure, they might not see all the executive-level complexities, but that's not their job. It's your job as a leader to take those raw ideas and mould them into something actionable. Instead of shutting it down, listen and work with them. A suggestion that feels misaligned at first could hold a kernel of truth that sparks real improvement when coached properly. The worst thing you can do is ask for ideas and then fail to act on them...or worse, shut them down without explanation. That doesn't just discourage people from speaking up; it erodes trust. And without trust, the bottom-up approach falls apart.

Here's the reality: if you're not prepared to genuinely consider suggestions, you're better off not asking for them in the first place. Soliciting ideas only to ignore them sends a clear message: we don't really value what you have to say. That's a fast track to disengagement. On the flip side, when you take the time to listen, refine, and align those suggestions with the bigger picture, you create a culture of collaboration and ownership. Even if a suggestion doesn't make the final cut, showing the crew that their voices are heard and respected builds loyalty and fosters innovation.

This is why Toyota are considered legends in culture. This isn't just efficiency; it's culture. It's a way of saying, "We see you, we trust you, and your contribution matters". And the results? Toyota is renowned not only for the quality of its products but also for the loyalty and engagement of its workforce. The company sweats the small stuff, and that small stuff adds up to something incredible over time.

That's the kind of culture we're striving to build. A culture where every detail matters, where no issue is too minor to address, and where every person feels empowered to contribute. Because we know that the smallest ideas, when nurtured, can often have the biggest impact. Sweating the small stuff doesn't just mean fixing tiny imperfections. It's about creating a workplace where people are proud to bring their ideas forward because they know those ideas will be valued.

Sitting on a Couch With a Stripper

The sun was brutal that January day, the kind of heat that turns industrial warehouses into human frying pans. I was drenched in sweat, holed up in the warehouse waiting for the air conditioner to kick in. I was in the office early, not just for the meeting itself that I'd scheduled, but to go over and be laser focused on the biggest quote of my career. A retirement village contract...a gateway to the big leagues of commercial painting. But also, a loaded gun that could blow the whole operation if mishandled.

I'd spent weeks with our estimator combing through every square metre, every hidden corner, every possible pitfall. This wasn't just guesswork; this year was years of incremental gains in action. We'd developed our square metre rates for each surface over years down to the decimal point. Over time, we'd built a quoting process as precise as possible. A capability statement to sell our quality and process, risk assessments that accounted for weather, coverage issues of colours, are there deadlines that might force us to work overtime, cutting into our profit? Admin overloads, and even how many coffees our supervisor might need to keep sane.

This wasn't always the case. There were times we underquoted and took the financial gut punch, learning the hard way. But now, each misstep had been forged into a better system. When I hit submit, I wasn't thinking, what if we've fucked this up? My thought was, no one has done the prep we've done, and we've done all we can. I confidently hit submit.

The meeting hadn't officially started yet, but the crew was already gathering, milling around the pool table as someone racked the balls. The low hum of chatter filled the room, mixed with the clatter of pool cues and the occasional burst of laughter. It was one of those casual pre-meeting moments...half gossip, half caffeine-fuelled catch-up. The summer break had clearly left everyone with stories to tell.

"Mate, you're still red as a lobster," one of the young guys said, nudging Max, who was peeling from his obvious sunburn.

"Yeah, yeah, I snoozed for too long at the beach yesterday, was a bit tired from Saturday night," Max replied, running a hand over his neck. "Anyway, you want to hear what happened at the bucks I went to?"

A few of the guys perked up, leaning in. "What'd you do, get kicked out of somewhere?"

"Nah, worse," Max said, a grin spreading across his face. "So, I had cricket all day and missed most of it. The plan was for me to meet them at the last venue. I rock up, right? And guess what? The boys are still an hour away."

"Classic," someone chimed in. "Bet you started sinking beers to catch up."

"Yeah, the last venue was just back at one of the boy's houses, so I just grabbed a beer and waited on the couch." Max said, shaking his head. "Anyway, this girl rocked up. I just assumed it was just one of the guy's wives. I was a bit confused why she was here, but I didn't really know what they'd organised."

The room erupted into laughter, the kind that has everyone struggling to breathe.

"Was she a stripper?" one of the guys spluttered, barely holding onto his coffee. "What'd you say to her? 'So, uh, come here often?'"

"She was actually pretty chill," Max said, barely able to finish his sentence through his own laughter. "We talked about her dog! Her dog! Like, what the hell else was I supposed to do? The boys were nowhere to be found."

Another guy wiped tears from his eyes. "Mate, you've just set a new bar for awkward situations. Imagine the look on her face. 'This bloke is more interested in my golden retriever than anything else.'"

The whole crew was in stitches, leaning on chairs and clutching their sides. It was the perfect icebreaker before the meeting got underway...proof that nothing beats the camaraderie of shared laughter over ridiculous summer antics.

Meanwhile, Jason sauntered in, already red-faced but not from the heat. He was the type of guy who you could explain something to three times, and he'd still act like you were speaking German. He was also convinced he knew more than anyone else at any given time.

My presentation was locked and loaded; a recap of the year behind us and our roadmap for the year ahead, including a shiny new project management app we'd spent months investigating. It was the latest in our arsenal of marginal gains. One of the office guys had been tasked with reviewing, trailing, and reporting on countless apps before presenting findings to me, not leaving anything to chance. This wasn't just about convenience; it was about setting a standard for efficiency and quality in the year ahead.

This wasn't an open-forum, pipe-up-when-you-want style meeting like an Ask Me Anything, nor was it a free-flowing town hall. It was structured...me going through a presentation. Questions and discussions were for later, after I'd finished. I wanted the team to understand the roadmap without getting derailed by tangents.

But, of course, every team has a Jason. The guy who thinks he knows better than anyone, the one who'd tell a Michelin-star chef their steak was overcooked or a barista that their latte art lacked creativity...cue Jason.

Halfway through the presentation, right when I was hitting my stride, he leaned back in his chair, arms crossed and interrupted. "Oi, have you tried the app Tradify? I heard about it on Triple M. Way better than this system you're showing us."

The room fell silent, heads turning toward him as I paused, mid-slide, staring at the chart I'd just painstakingly explained.

"Thanks, Jason," I said, forcing a tight smile. "But you think I haven't thought of that? Just listen to what I'm about to say."

Now this Tradify app? We've looked at it. Thoroughly. It wasn't for us. And in the heat of the moment, the morning stress, the heat, I shut him down a bit too hard, more general shutting up of dumb ideas than constructive leadership. Regret set in immediately.

See, Jason's suggestion wasn't great. But in squashing it like that, I risked silencing someone else with a killer idea. I should have said, "Jason, love that you're thinking. We reviewed that one and decided on this after a lot of testing. Let's work together to master it."

It wasn't about Jason's app; it was about showing the crew their voice mattered. Every idea, no matter how off-base, could spark something great. Marginal gains aren't just about processes or products...they're about culture. You win by making everyone feel they're apart of the journey, that their contributions move the needle. And that day, I failed at that part.

So, while I nailed the quote prep with years of refined systems (we went on to win that tender), I did, however, fumble the team dynamic in that team meeting. Both were lessons in marginal gains... one about the importance of preparation, the other about ensuring every person feels like they are a part of the bigger picture. One step forward, one step back...but always learning.

CHAPTER 16

YOU DON'T GET BETTER AT HIRING, YOU GET BETTER AT FIRING

Steve Bartlett, in his podcast and book *The Diary of a CEO*, introduces a straightforward yet profound graph to evaluate employees: Exceeding Expectations, Neutral, and Not Improving the Company. The message is simple: if someone consistently falls into the last category, it's time to let them go. This aligns with the philosophy that we may not get significantly better at hiring; but we can sharpen our ability to make timely decisions about moving on from the wrong people. It's about understanding that keeping someone who isn't contributing can cause more harm than letting them go.

He often says you don't get better at hiring; you get better at firing. It's a humbling truth, especially for anyone who's ever hired someone and felt their ego tied to that decision. "I hired this person, so I need to make it work" becomes a trap. But hiring is hard...sometimes borderline impossible to get right. Interviews can only reveal so much, and the reality is, you'll often get it wrong. For us, hiring a painter can feel like a game of endurance. Forty people applied. Ten make the shortlist. Six answer the phone. Four are worth interviewing. Three show up. Two are good enough for a trial. And only one sticks. It's more about resilience than precision. The key is not to cling to the idea of being right but to recognise when you've made the wrong call and act on it quickly. Letting someone go isn't easy, but it's often the most honest and fair decision for them and the team.

I still remember the most impressive interview I've ever sat in. It was recent, and at that point, I was feeling pretty confident in my ability to read people. The guy was fresh out of the AFL system, had done some landscaping, and was coaching VFL on the side. He said painting was what he truly wanted to do. He'd researched the business, understood what we were about, and spoke about bringing his elite sporting mindset to our team. He'd tasted professional environments, bounced back from the heartbreak of an AFL career cut short, and, as if he needed bonus points... had played for my beloved Bulldogs.

He was confident without being cocky, spoke well, and seemed genuinely passionate about the trade. I walked out of that interview so impressed I'm surprised I didn't offer him a stake in the company on the spot. I hired him immediately. No trial, no hesitation. I spent that weekend at a BBQ bragging about him like I'd just pulled off a masterstroke.

Then one of my mates overheard and asked for his name. He'd worked with him before... same guy, same backstory. "Mate, that bloke's the sketchiest person I've ever worked with. He's a compulsive liar. Won my old boss over too with the smooth talk. Worst labourer we've ever had. And I've lost count of how many times his grandpa's apparently died."

I was stunned. "Nah, different guy," I said. "Nope," he replied. "That's him. Doesn't want to be a painter... just got sacked from landscaping. His latest lie was that he had stage 4 cancer."

I called the guy that night and withdrew the offer.

A few years later I bumped into him at a bakery in Collingwood. Still talking smooth, still selling the dream. Since our interview, he'd churned through more than ten jobs, multiple girlfriends, and a few different footy clubs. Nothing had stuck.

It was a sharp reminder that charisma isn't character. It also taught me not to let my ego – or my soft spot for the Doggies – cloud my judgement. I wanted it to be a great hire so badly that I ignored the need for verification, reference checks, or even a trial. I was invested in being right.

That's the real trap. You don't get better at hiring. You just get better at identifying when it's not working... and acting fast, before the damage spreads.

When I was coaching football, I had a mantra of seeing the positives: focus on what players can do, rather than what they can't. It's a philosophy I believed in deeply. That was the hill I chose to die on. But here's the thing: while it sounded noble, it became a slippery slope. I started letting too much slide, focusing so hard on potential that I began accepting mediocrity. Sure, I had hard non-negotiables. But the silent underminers, the ones who weren't overly toxic but quietly eroded the team? They were harder to call out and even harder to manage.

Interestingly, the mantra of focusing on strengths has proven incredibly effective in elite-level sport recently. Take Chris Fagan, the Brisbane Lions coach, for example. Fagan often cops criticism for not being as tactical as his contemporaries. He's not the type to swing the magnets or overcomplicate his strategy when his players are struggling. Instead, he backs his players to dig deep and turn things around themselves. Analysts like David King might jump on talkback radio to critique his lack of coaching nuance, but Fagan's approach creates an incredible sense of belief within his team.

Imagine being a player under Fagan...knowing that your coach will stand by you, even when things get tough...especially if things get tough. That kind of confidence can't be quantified, and it's no coincidence that the Brisbane Lions are the reigning AFL premiers and of the most successful teams in the past decade.

A similar philosophy underpins the success of Andrew McDonald, the current Australian cricket coach. Cricket selection in Australia is a national obsession...a rite of passage! Pundits, fans, and former players endlessly debate who should be in the XI. But McDonald doesn't let the noise penetrate his team. He backs his players unconditionally, giving them the room to perform without the fear of being dropped at the first sign of trouble. And the results speak for themselves; at the time of writing, the Australian cricket holds every bilateral trophy, the ICC World Cup, and the Test Championship. They've won nearly everything there is to win. That's the power of belief and stability in leadership...it fosters loyalty and inspires them to perform.

The flip side to focusing on what people can do is that it can create blind spots. Backing someone purely on potential, without addressing gaps or accountability, can erode team standards. As a leader, the challenge is to balance optimism with realism: to believe in people without letting mediocrity slip through the cracks.

But then, there's a third flip side to this philosophy, if such a thing even exists. I'm not coaching the Australian Cricket Team...though I did captain a backyard cricket team to championship amongst my mates. Nor am I leading a professional AFL squad. I'm running a small painting company. The stakes are different. My team isn't being scrutinised by the nation on talkback radio, and I don't have a squad of highly paid players on long-term contracts. If someone isn't cutting it in my crew, it's not just about performance...it's about the survival and culture of the business. Every hire has an outsized impact, and every mistake carries a heavier cost.

Backing someone who isn't delivering...whether through misplaced belief or reluctance to let them go, can feel like dragging an anchor behind you. The business suffers, and the rest of the team feels it. In an elite sports team, one underperforming player can often be carried by others. In a small company, one weak link can bring everything to a standstill.

Of course, retention is still critical. Losing an employee costs time, money, and momentum. Studies show replacing an employee cost, on average, 20% of their salary. In a small business, where budgets are tight and every hour counts, those costs sting even more. That's why investing in retention, focusing on employee happiness, engagement, and development...is essential. A happy team performs better, stays longer, and builds a stronger culture.

But the key is finding the balance. Retention can't come at the cost of standards. It's a tightrope act: knowing when to back someone in and knowing when to move them out. Sometimes, the best decision for the business is letting someone go...not just for the team, but for them too. If someone isn't thriving, maybe they're in the wrong role, the wrong environment, or the wrong team.

So, while admiring the philosophies of leaders like Chris Fagan and Andrew McDonald, I also must ground those lessons in my reality. Running a small business requires a different kind of balance...a mix of belief, accountability, and pragmatism. Confidence is powerful, but standards are non-negotiable. And the best leaders, whether in sport or business, know how to walk that line.

Cut 'Em Loose

Leadership, particularly in small business, is a minefield of tough calls. The hardest decisions aren't just about numbers...they're about people. Balancing someone's strengths against their weaknesses, deciding whether to back them in or move them on, requires a mix of principles, gut instinct and experience.

I've faced this challenge with several team members over the years. Each situation was different, yet that all came down to the same question:

If they quit tomorrow, would I be relieved?

Would I hire them again?

If the answers to those questions are yes and no, respectively, the path becomes clear, even if it's not easy. Let me break down with some real-life examples.

The Toxic Speed Demon

This guy was lightning on the brush...efficient, precise and fast. If you needed a house painted in record time with the highest quality, he was your man. A rare painting unicorn. But everything else? A complete trainwreck. He was the team gossip, constantly stirring up drama and creating divisions. He wasn't a glass half full guy; he was glass empty. He ran his job site with a sad pessimism that life was the worst...he was a dementor sucking the life out of his teammates. We got a new warehouse; it was a lot smaller than he thought. A new apprentice starts full of optimism and energy; he doesn't even know what a sash on a window means. You'd put on free drinks at the Christmas party; the venue was a bit crowded. You'd write up a congratulation message on Slack highlighting the good work that someone has done; he'll comment, 'about time they pulled their finger out'. We all know the type.

The problem wasn't just his negativity...it was the impact that it had on the team. His negativity was contagious, pulling others into his complaints and undermining the culture we were building. I'd talk to him, wrap my arms around him, pump him up, try redirect his energy. Nothing stuck.

His talent made it hard to let go. He was so quick, and in a trade where time is money, that mattered. If I moved him, tangibly speaking, we would lose money, right? But here's the truth...speed doesn't outweigh toxicity. f someone is dragging the team down, their strengths don't matter. I realised that keeping him on was costing us more in morale than his efficiency was saving us time.

The Charismatic Slacker (with a side story about my ute getting stolen)

Then there was the funny guy. Smart, charming, the life of the party. Everyone loved him, me included. He had this way of lighting the mood, of making the hardest days feel easier. He was also highly skilled in ways that made your jaw drop. He picked up spraying faster than anyone I've seen...what took others a year to master, he had it down in a week And it wasn't just spraying. He was a natural. Fancy knots? He knew them all, like he'd been a sailor in another life. Backing a trailer? Not a problem. I once saw him whip a trailer into a tight spot so casually, it was like he'd done it a thousand times blindfolded.

And he had a knack for the trade lingo, too. One trip to the paint shop and he could rattle off the product lines like he'd been working for them for years. Lustacryl, Enamacryl, Low Sheen, Lustaglow, Lumbersider, Spacecote, Hi-glow. You name it, he knew it. And he didn't just know it...he made an impression. He'd charm whoever was behind the counter, guy or girl, leaving them grinning like they'd just met their new best friend. Even The Toxic Speed Demon couldn't bring himself to say a bad word about him. That's how good he could be.

But beneath the humour, there were issues.

He was chronically late, his timesheets were...creative, and his back conveniently acted up most Mondays. He was a master at skating by...just enough effort to stay under the radar but never enough to truly contribute. I kept thinking, he'll turn it around. He's too smart not to. But he never did.

On a side note, good time to wedge in a funny story. This was the same bloke who once stole my ute right out of my driveway as a joke. He'd driven past my house, noticed the keys were in it, and thought, why not? He jumped in, parked it around the corner, then sat back and watched me freak out, convinced my car had been stolen. Years later, he was still working with us when my actual car did get stolen. It's the weirdest feeling...you lose all logic. I walked the block, trying to convince myself I'd parked it somewhere else, even though I knew damn well I hadn't. Eventually, I rang him.

"Remember when you stole my car a few years ago as a joke? You didn't happen to do that again, did you?"

Unfortunately, the answer was no. This time, my car really was gone. I'd never been a big car guy, but this was my first-ever brand-new car, and just a few months in, it'd bloody been pinched. Over the next few weeks, I had friends messaging me and Edwina, saying, "Someone's hooning around in a Paint It Black car. Didn't look like Josh." Funny thing was, at the time, we had about eight cars on the road, so I kept getting calls, "Found your car, mate. It's on the coast." Every time, it was just another one of our work vehicles. I reckon I had more updates on our fleet's whereabouts in those weeks than I'd had in the past year.

Insurance eventually covered it, and I'm pretty sure I left my golf clubs in the back (wink wink), so at least I got a new set out of it. Didn't help my game, though. Anyway, I've gone completely off track here, but that's the type of prankster we're dealing with.

I let him slide longer than I should have because I liked him, and I wanted him to succeed. But being liked isn't the same as being valuable. The Charismatic Slacker had the tools to be one of the best. But in the end, it's not about what someone can do. It's about what they will do, day in and day out.

When I finally asked myself the two questions, the answers were obvious: yes, I'd be relieved if he left, and no, I wouldn't hire him again. That told me everything I needed to know.

The Promising Apprentice

Then there was a girl, full of promise. She started out strong... eager, talented, with a great attitude. Clients loved her...truly loved her. They'd go out of their way to request her by name for repeat jobs, always singing her praises. They'd rave about her work ethic, her attention to detail, and how easy it was to communicate with her. She wasn't just about making promises...she acted on them, consistently delivering without needing to be reminded. Feedback? She took it in her stride, using it to fuel her improvement. She wasn't the type to talk a big game; she was all about showing results.

But then punctuality issues started creeping in, along with flaky excuses for days off. It was frustrating because I could see the potential, but her reliability was slipping.

Unlike the other two, her behaviour wasn't toxic. It felt...off. So, we did what we always try to do in these situations: I asked if everything was okay...outside of work. Although she brushed it off at the time, it turned out, she was dealing with a lot at home. Personal issues were spilling over into work.

The difference with her was ownership. She didn't make excuses or play the victim. And she did slip up a few times after. When I gave her tough love, she took it on board. When I offered her support, she appreciated it. She admitted her mistakes and worked to fix them.

It wasn't a smooth ride...there were more spikes in performance and moments of doubt. But she pulled through. By the end of her apprenticeship, she had not only earned back my trust but had also become a supervisor and a key part of the team.

These three stories highlight the fine line leaders must walk. Do you back them and risk the team? Or do you cut them loose and risk losing potential? There's no formula for this...every person, every situation, is different. But sticking to your core philosophies helps.

For me, it comes down to this: if someone isn't moving the needle forward, they're holding the team back. And the longer you let it slide, the harder it gets to fix. But at the same time, you must balance accountability with empathy. People make mistakes. Life happens. The key is to differentiate between those who won their mistakes and those who deflect them. A good worker is someone who takes a little more of their share of the blame and a little less of their share of the credit.

I'm not running the Australian Cricket Team or the Brisbane Lions. I don't have a deep bunch of talent to call up at a moment's notice. But the principles of leadership are the same at every level:

Set clear standards and stick to them. Letting things slide, even for talented people, undermines the whole team.

Balance empathy with accountability. Support people through tough times, but don't tolerate excuses or repeated issues.

Trust your gut and your moral compass. Those two questions — Would you be relieved if they quit? Would you hire them again? Sometimes it means letting them go. Either way, you've got to stay true to your values.

Continuing with the Brisbane Lions theme, their famous coach of the early 2000s, Leigh Matthews, has a famous line, *"You treat everyone fairly, but not exactly equally,"* has always struck me as an essential truth when it comes to managing talent. There's a natural tendency to give more leg rope to people who show raw potential. Talent, after all, buys you time. If someone can perform at a high level, even if they're a bit rough around the edges, you're inclined to give them more chances, more patience. You can overlook a lot of flaws when the person has spark, that promise. But here's the kicker...that grace period doesn't last forever.

In the real world, time eventually runs out...even for the most gifted. Eventually, you need to ask yourself if the potential is turning into actual results or if the talent is just an excuse for poor performance. The charismatic slacker might pick up spraying in a week, charm the paint shop staff with ease, and be faster than anyone on the job, but at some point, his inability to follow through or his lack of consistency will catch up with him. The client might love him, but the cracks start to show. It's one thing to give someone a break because they're talented, but there comes a time when the patience wears thin, and the line must be drawn.

That's when the real test comes. Are you willing to make the hard call, to let go of the person with the big promise because they are no longer pulling their weight? Because no matter how much leg rope you give them, they're still holding back the team if they don't change. At some point, the decision becomes clear: do they deserve the extra time? Or is it time to move on.

In the end, it's about balance. You want to give your talented people every chance to succeed, but you can't let them slide forever. Time may have bought them some space, but that doesn't mean you wait around indefinitely. Talent must translate into results, and if it doesn't, that's when you must ask the hard questions.

CHAPTER 17

IF YOU KNEW THE ENDING, WOULD YOU BOTHER TURNING THE PAGE?

In business, building a successful team is less about perfect strategies and more about the people executing them. The foundation of any great organisation lies in this simple truth: hire for attitude, train for skill, and make sure the right people are in the right seats.

Why attitude? Because skills can be developed, but values like adaptability, resilience, and a strong work ethic are harder to teach. A great hire isn't just someone with a stellar resume...it's someone who aligns with your company's culture and beliefs. They bring energy, positivity, and a willingness to learn. On the flip side, a bad attitude can erode team morale faster than you realize.

The right seats approach stems from Jim Collins' famous book, Good to Great, where he emphasises that a company's success isn't solely based on strategy. Instead, it's about assembling the right team and allowing them to drive the bus, even if you're figuring out the exact destination.

When you think about your team, you can usually spot the difference between the 'show horses' and the 'plow horses'. Show horses love the spotlight...they're flashy and impressive at first but often disappear when it's time to do the grind. Plow horses, however, are the backbone of your business. They quietly show up, shoulder the load, and consistently deliver. These are the people who drive long-term success.

The key to building a winning team is prioritising the plow horses. If you find yourself needing to tightly manage someone...reminders, handholding, or micromanaging, it's a red flag. The best employees manage themselves. They take ownership, solve problems, and seek feedback to improve. That's not to say they don't need guidance or mentorship; everyone does. But the distinction is clear...supporting someone's growth is vastly different from having to carry them. If someone requires excessive oversight, they're draining resources that could be better spent elsewhere. The best teams are made up of self-starters who thrive with a little autonomy and trust.

The litmus test. When evaluating someone's place on the team, ask yourself this tough but revealing question: would I hire this person again? If your answer isn't an immediate and resounding yes, it's time to dig deeper. Trust your instincts. Ask yourself another question: would you feel relieved or secretly happy if they left your team? If your answer is yes, that's your gut telling you something important...they're not the right fit.

But building a strong team isn't just about hiring great people...it's about putting them in roles that leverage their strengths. A plow horse in the wrong seat can become frustrated and unproductive. But when you align someone's strengths with their responsibilities, they thrive...and so does your business.

This principle became painfully clear to us once. We had a talented team member in a role that didn't suit their abilities. It wasn't that they weren't capable...they just weren't in the right seat. Once we reassessed and made the shift, their performance skyrocketed, and their satisfaction with the role did too. It's a reminder that the right people in the wrong roles are still a liability.

The importance of having the right people on the bus is just as important as getting the wrong people off the bus. Having the wrong people on the bus doesn't just harm the team's efficiency; they also disrupt morale and weaken the culture. Keeping someone on board who doesn't align with your vision, values, or work ethic, doesn't just hold them back...it holds the whole team back. It's a tough call to make, but removing the wrong people creates space for the right people to thrive.

This approach isn't about being ruthless; it's about being honest... with yourself, your team, and the individual in question. It's not fair to keep someone in a role when they're not thriving or contributing effectively. And it's certainly not fair to your team to keep carrying dead weight.

And what happens when you don't execute this well? The cracks show, often at the worst times. Jim Collins provides an example in Good to Great about two banks. One was obsessed with perfect strategies, KPIs, and plans. The other focused on hiring exceptional people and ensuring the wrong ones didn't stick around. They'd often hire exceptional people even without a particular role in mind. When an unforeseen crisis hit the banking sector, the first bank's rigid strategy fell apart, while the second thrived because of its adaptable, capable team. The takeaway is simple: strategy is only as strong as the people executing it.

In business, as in life, it's the journey...not the destination, that matters. Focusing on the process, the execution, and the relationships you build along the way is far more rewarding than obsessing over a single goal or end point. Having the right people on your team makes the journey worthwhile and ensures you'll handle whatever twist comes your way. It's like reading a great book: if you knew the ending, would you even bother turning the page? The excitement, the growth, and the lessons all happen along the way. And when you prioritise people over strategy, you're building a team capable of navigating those chapters, no matter what story unfolds.

Cancel Culture? Or The Consequences of Someone's Actions?

This one sticks with me, not because it was easy, but because it was necessary. You could see it coming like a train in the distance, hoping that maybe it would switch tracks. But no, the writing was on the wall long before this final chapter played out. This guy? A true character. The type who could walk into a room and instantly fill it with laughter and energy. He had that magnetic charm...the kind that makes people naturally gravitate towards him. And yeah, I liked him too, how could you not? He even attended my wedding.

But there's a truth about charisma: it can carry you far, but not far enough to outrun poor judgement. And this guy? He crossed the line...not just once, but repeatedly. I'd pulled him aside for a couple of those, "Mate, you can't say that" conversations. They weren't aggressive or heavy-handed; they were direct but still compassionate. Each time, I hoped it would click for him. But charm, unfortunately, doesn't equate to change.

The last straw was one of them moments when you realise that there is no coming back. His comments had gone from inappropriate to outright unacceptable. I remember the final conversation vividly.

It's the kind of pending conversation that keeps you up the night before...a weight in your chest, an ache in your gut. I've had tough conversations before, and they are nearly always easier than you've built up in your head. But that doesn't make the dread go away. No matter how many times you rehearse it in your head, you know it won't feel natural when the time comes. That's how I felt driving to the meeting, coffee in hand, heart pounding. I was nervous, no doubt about it. I'd sacked plenty of people before for things that were black and white...racism, sexism, homophobia. No hesitation, no second thoughts. But this? This was different. It wasn't one glaring incident; it was a slow buildup of little things, a death by a thousand cuts to the team culture.

I've had to let people go before for poor performance or other reasons, but this situation was different. In the past, there was a time when sacking someone was almost straightforward...a low hanging fruit, so to speak. There was one apprentice, for instance, who had a bit of a habit of saying some ignorant things. One incident stuck out: she made a comment to an Indigenous teammate that was completely inappropriate. It wasn't malicious, just ignorant, but that didn't make it acceptable.

It wasn't the first time she said something out of line either. She wasn't performing well in her role, and to be honest, she was lucky to still have a job at that point. So, when that incident happened, I made a call to let her go. It was a clear message to the rest of the crew: zero tolerance. The standards were non-negotiable, and her departure served as a reminder for that.

But this? This was different. This wasn't an underperforming apprentice. Yes, that time might have sent a bit of a statement to the crew, but as I said, it was a bit of a low hanging fruit, and nobody was really surprised or rocked by it. This upcoming conversation, however, was one of our most experienced painters...a supervisor, no less. Someone I'd trusted with our most prestigious jobs. An exceptional painter who had taught me so much over the years. In fact, a lot of these lessons I've written in here, I learned from him. This wasn't someone who was skating unnoticed. This was a core team member, a big personality, and someone who'd contributed significantly to my career and to the success of the company.

I stopped by Roscoe's Social Club that morning, my usual coffee spot in Geelong, and chatted to Ross, the owner. Normally, I'd have been thrilled to catch up. He'd fill me in on any hilarious life mishaps his younger brother, my old housemate, Cameron has had. But that day, I could barely string a coherent thought together. My mind was already at the meeting, rehearsing what I'd say and how I'd say it. Even the coffee tasted off, like my taste buds had gone on strike, knowing what was coming.

When I finally sat him down, I could feel my hands gripping the chair tighter than they needed to, like I was bracing for a storm. He had that easy grin, the kind that had gotten him out of trouble dozens of times before. I had chosen the lunch area for the talk. I have no idea why...maybe the office felt too formal, too much of an execution, step into my office...it felt off. More likely I just wanted it over and the walk up the stairs added an extra 60 seconds of dread. I sat on one of the stools, up against the high table. I don't remember asking him to sit...I do remember him standing, fidgeting. The warehouse is normally very clean as far as warehouses go, but today it felt a bit cluttered, a bit messy...a metaphor for what was happening. There was a faint smell of paint from the previous day, somebody had been here spraying out some doors. There were a couple of coffee cups that hadn't been washed, some scaffold dropped off and not stacked correctly, and a big order of paint just arrived. "Just leave it under the stairs," I said a little too aggressively to the courier. Meanwhile, we just sat/stood there awkwardly until he finished unloading.

My palms were clammy, and I let out a slow, deliberate breath, trying to settle my nerves. "Mate," he said, still standing, crossing his arms. "What's this about? You're not still on about that comment, are ya? It was just banter. Locker room chat, you know how it is." His voice was casual, dismissive, like we were mates sharing a laugh over a beer.

I looked over at the paint that had just got delivered, and then quickly forced myself to hold his gaze, even though every part of me wanted to look away. I'd rehearsed this and could feel the words rising in my chest. I couldn't back down...don't be a coward.

"Mate, we've talked about this," I began, my voice steadier than I expected, though my throat felt tight. "I feel like I have a decent moral compass. Banter's part of the job sometimes. But this? It's not just one comment. It's the accumulation. You've crossed the line too many times."

His grin faltered, replaced by a flicker of disbelief. "Come on," he said, leaning forward, his tone almost pleading now. "Don't make this a big deal. You're blowing it out of proportion."

I shook my head, feeling a sharp knot form in my gut. "No," I said firmly, "I'm not. This isn't just about one thing. It's about how we treat each other. And when you act like that, you don't just let yourself down...you let me down."

That last bit hurt him, I could tell. And I wanted to take it back...but he did let me down. So, I stopped myself from talking, let that hang in the air for a bit longer. He stood up straight, his arms crossing again, but this time there was no grin, just a stubborn defiance. "What if I work on my own for a bit?" "No." "I'll just have a couple weeks off and re-set...can work away when I'm back?" "No, you no longer work here."

We looked at the ground for what felt like an eternity, not saying anything. I just wanted to be nice to him, but I couldn't back down at that moment. "Cancel culture got me," he finally muttered, shaking his head in frustration.

For a moment, the absurdity of his comment nearly broke my composure. I wanted to laugh, to roll my eyes, to snap back with something cutting. But I didn't. I just let the silence stretch between us, heavy and charged.

"No," I said finally, my voice starting to get a bit shaky. "This isn't cancel culture, mate. This is consequences of your actions."

The words hung in the air like the echo of a dropped hammer, final and undeniable. I surprised myself to be honest. Maybe I was angry. Looking back, I deserved to be too. Not only had he been a real cultural liability for quite a while, but he'd also put me in this position. He didn't argue anymore, just stared at the table, the defiance in his eyes softening into something that looked almost like regret.

When it was over, and he walked out of the warehouse, the heavy door clanging shut behind him, I leaned back in the chair and let out a long breath I didn't realise I'd been holding. My hands were stiff from how tightly I'd been gripping the chair, and my heart was racing, but there was a strange sense of calm settling in now. It wasn't easy, and it didn't feel good. But it felt right.

The rest of the day felt surreal, like I was moving through fog. After the meeting, I went to the driving range to clear my head, but it was like I'd forgotten to swing a club. Shank after shank, balls flying in every direction...nothing out of the ordinary really. The follow up calls were worse, the awkward echoes of a breakup. "I've got your drop sheets," he'd say, "Where are you? I'll drop them off." It felt hollow, transactional, like we both knew this was the end of something that had once been good.

I felt awful...absolutely gutted. This wasn't just a colleague; this was a mate, someone who'd lit up every room he walked into. But no amount of charisma could erase the damage he'd done to the team. And that's the thing about holding people accountable...you don't always walk away feeling like a hero. Sometimes you walk away with a knot in your stomach and the sound of their footsteps fading into the distance. But if you don't stand firm on what matters, the culture crumbles. And culture, more than anything else, is worth protecting.

Looking back, it reinforced a rule I hold tightly: no tolerance for crossing certain lines. Racist, sexist, or homophobic behaviour? You're gone, no hesitation. But this situation taught me there's another, more cloudy line...what I call the don't be a dickhead policy. It's harder to define, but just as important to uphold.

In the end, it wasn't about me or him...it was about the team. Protecting the culture means making tough calls, even when they hurt. Because when you let things slide...stick your head in the ground like an ostrich, you're sending a message...standards don't matter. And that's a slippery slope no team can afford.

In the end, he turned out fine. After I let him go, he went back to working for himself. It was a better fit for him. Over time, his cheeky humour started to come back in the conversations we'd have. He'd still call me from time to time, asking for advice about jobs, clients, or just hanging shit on me. There was a bit of remorse in his voice every now and again.

"Maybe I wasn't cut out for the bigger team," he admitted once, with that self-deprecating grin I could almost hear over the phone. And you know what? That's okay. Not everyone is meant to thrive in a structured team environment, and sometimes it takes a tough lesson to figure that out.

The funny thing? The apprentice I let go...the one who couldn't keep her foot out of her mouth...she ended up working for him. I'd teed it up before I let her go, knowing it might work out better for both. Full circle, right? Now they can say whatever inappropriate things they want together. Cancel culture won't come for them.

She even told a few of our workers that she'd been poached by him, which gave me a laugh. Poached! I mean, technically true, but the irony wasn't lost on anyone.

So yeah, this one was rough. But it was necessary. And as much as I hate how it played out, I walked away knowing I'd done the right thing. Dumbledore's words once again rung in my ears – you must do what is right, not what is easy.

CONCLUSION

KING REGARDS,
JOSH BLACK

If there's one thing I hope this book leaves you with, it's that there's no perfect way to do business...or life. You're going to make mistakes. You're going to get things wrong. And that's fine, as long as you're doing it your way. If you try to be someone else, you'll end up a poor version of them, and people will see straight through it. But if you back yourself, stay true to who you are, and own your journey... failures and all...you'll always be moving in the right direction.

At times, it'll feel overwhelming. There'll be days where everything goes wrong, where the weight of running a business feels unbearable. But when that happens, take a step back and get some perspective. When my son, Vinny, is having a rough day (which, to be fair, isn't often, he's bloody adorable), I remind myself that others have it much harder. Edwina's sister had three kids under two, including twins. There are parents doing it alone, without support, or dealing with things far tougher than a bit of broken sleep. And suddenly, my problems don't seem so big. Business is the same. You're not the first person to deal with difficult clients, cash flow headaches, or a project that's gone completely sideways. These mistakes have been made before, and they'll be made again. The key is to learn from them and keep moving forward.

There's no magic formula to success...just bloody hard work. The more effort you put in, the more capable and confident you become. And confidence makes everything easier. It helps you make decisions with conviction, take risks without fear, and trust in your ability to figure things out.

But the most important thing? Don't forget why you started in the first place. Your business should support your life, not consume it. The real measure of success isn't just money – it's time. Time to do the things you love, be with the people who matter, and enjoy the journey. Because at the end of the day, we only get one shot at this. So, work hard, stay true to yourself, and don't take it all too seriously.

King Regards,

Josh Black.

ABOUT THE AUTHOR

Josh Black doesn't see himself as a writer. He doesn't even consider himself much of a businessman, though he's managed to run Paint It Black for over 10 years. What Josh really is, is someone who can't sit still...someone who loves the energy of building and growing a business.

Living in Collingwood with his wife, Edwina, and son, Vinny, Josh has a lot of passions. You'l often find him on the golf course, glued to the Bulldogs game, or grabbing a beer at one of the many local breweries in Collingwood.

With no formal qualifications, Josh's expertise comes from learning through real-world experience. Paint It Black has been built on lessons learned from mistakes, and those lessons are the foundation of the company's culture. Josh believes that business is about creating something meaningful with good people, and that small businesses deserve to have their voices heard in a world dominated by big corporations.

For more about Josh and his work, visit www.paintitblack.online.

NOTES

- King Henry VIII had 6 wives and beheaded two

- The dartboard line is called an oche

- Black pepper and cumin are the two-best selling peppers

- The Cambodian alphabet is the longest in the world with 76 letters

- Don't be a ostrich (stick your head in the sand and hope the problem goes away)

_____

_____

_____

_____

_____

_____

ACCIDENTALLY IN CHARGE

_____

_____

_____

_____

_____

_____

_____

_____

_____

_____

_____

_____

_____

_____

_____

NOTES

ACCIDENTALLY IN CHARGE

NOTES